Seeking Light

Light

The Esoteric Heart of Freemasonry

Michael R. Poll

Seeking Light
The Esoteric Heart of Freemasonry
by Michael R. Poll

A Cornerstone Book
Published by Cornerstone Book Publishers
Copyright © 2015, 2021, 2023 by Michael R. Poll

Cornerstone Book Publishers
Hot Springs Village, AR

First Cornerstone Edition - 2015
Second Cornerstone Edition – 2021
Third Cornerstone Edition - 2023

www.cornerstonepublishers.com

Table of Contents

Alice came to a fork in the road. "Which road do I take?" she asked.
"Where do you want to go?" responded the Cheshire cat.
"I don't know," Alice answered.
"Then," said the cat, "it doesn't matter.

~ Lewis Carroll, *Alice in Wonderland*

Introduction

Who are we, what are we, and where are we going? That's certainly a series of questions to stop most thoughtful people in their tracks. For that matter, what is Freemasonry? We'll explore some of these questions within the following pages and express some thoughts on these and other matters. A few of the subjects might be alien and strange to some readers, but once introduced and you get to know them a bit, you may become very good friends.

But there is no need to push or struggle with foreign concepts. Not every path is for every traveler. This is not a book of laws. No one should ever expect another to accept what is, for them, unacceptable. This is a book of considered thoughts and ideas written with the goal of assisting *me* as I travel down my own path. If my path happens to also be yours, join me! If my words provide you with some reason to stop and think, then I am happy. If this is not the book for you, keep searching for your path and accept my best thoughts and wishes.

As in all things Masonic, the goal is the search for Light.

Michael R. Poll
Fall, 2015

As far as we can discern, the sole purpose of existence is to kindle a light in the darkness of being.

~ Carl Jung

Seeking Light
The Esoteric Heart of Freemasonry

Living in a World of Change

"Everyone thinks of changing the world,
but no one thinks of changing himself."

~ Leo Tolstoy

For all our great achievements, man is a simple, lonely being. We are bound to the laws of nature just as the most uncomplicated and basic forms of life. When it rains, we get wet. When the temperature drops, we become cold. For all our self-professed intelligence, we live to a great extent at the mercy of the elements and are bound to natural laws which we hardly understand, much less control. We are egotistical slaves in the guise of masters.

But we do have a great ability. It is called free will. We have the power to use our minds and our actions (to the extent of their limits) in a manner of our choosing. We don't have to think evil (however we define that word). We don't have to do evil—unless that is what we choose to do. We can make choices. We can change how we think. We can improve our minds. Or, we can do nothing. Mahatma Gandhi wrote, "We must become the change we want to see." It does not best serve us to expect the world to change to suit our fancy. It also does not mean that if all around us is unsatisfactory, we must change to suit the fancy of others. We have the right to refuse

1

change forced upon us. Gandhi also wrote, "You can chain me, you can torture me, you can even destroy this body, but you will never imprison my mind." We must achieve a balance and a responsibility that we must assume, which goes along with free will.

Over the last dozen or so years, there has been a change in Masonry brewing. Books, research papers, and websites have been made available devoted to suggestions on ways that lodges can improve their operations and also to bring the Masonic lodge experience more in line with the views held by a growing number of Masons. It seems there is a desire in some to change. But is change universally desired?

In this paper, I will explore some of what might have taken place to bring us to this present situation and try to determine if there actually is a problem, what that problem might be, and any answers we might discover. The ultimate goal is to find a way for us to make the most out of our own Masonic lodge experience.

I imagine the best place to start is in the early days of what we know as Speculative Freemasonry. Going back to the days of the old Operative Freemasons may not be completely useful. While there is considerable evidence that this is where the inspiration for our present system can be found, our structure today is that of the Speculative Freemasonry that was created in the late 1600s and early 1700s. This is the model for today's Freemasonry. 1717 is the year that the Grand Lodge of England was created, but that was the result of events happening shortly before and, with some fine-tuning, a little after 1717. So, the late 1600s and early 1700s would be the best time frame for this discussion. And while there is much that we simply don't know from those early days, there is one thing that is clear — when Speculative Freemasonry was first presented to the world, it *was* popular. It took off much like wildfire. Whatever cord it struck with the masses, it was very much in tune with the desires of the people. It soon began spreading, and not only in England but everywhere. Today there is no corner of the world where freedom exists where you will not find Freemasonry. This is an example of the global and human attractiveness of Masonry.

For the first several hundred years after Speculative Masonry came to the notice of the world, lodge membership number was relatively small (by today's standards). If a lodge had 20 to 30 members, then it was considered a large lodge. If more members sought to join, then they would likely split to create a new lodge for the additional members. Smaller was considered the norm at that time.

While the lodges started out small in number and at a distance from each other, events began taking place in the mid-1900s, right after the end of World War II, that changed Freemasonry in the United States. Whereas lodges had been small, membership suddenly exploded. The numbers grew dramatically. Of course, it wasn't just Freemasonry but all societies and clubs in the U.S. saw dramatic membership spikes. It became the time of fraternal orders. Lodges and Grand Lodges could be seen as doubling and tripling in membership during this time. Why this happened is a matter of debate, but the fact is that lodges and Grand Lodges in the U.S. grew considerably, and all the new Masons needed to be accommodated. The many new members coming into Masonry provided a challenge for the Grand Lodges. Once where there had been a Grand Secretary and, maybe, an office secretary helping out, now entire office staffs were needed to manage the new communications, records, and other business of the increased membership. The same was true of the Grand Treasurer. Now, groups of accountants were needed to properly keep the books for all the new members. All of this was needed to keep the new and expanding *machine* that had been created working properly.

Grand Lodges suddenly found themselves with far more income from the new members, but this was offset by the new buildings that needed to be built and other expansions because of the growth. The dramatic increase in membership in U.S. Grand Lodges was not limited to any particular area, it was across the U.S.

My personal belief as to why this increase in members took place has to do with society following World War II. After years of hardship and war (and the period prior to it), there seems to have been a general feeling of prosperity and hope in America. Things were looking up, and everyone wanted to do things that were fun, entertaining, or relaxing.

I remember the Grand Lodge building in New Orleans, and for many years it was a center for Masonic and civic activity. My grandfather (whose lodge met in the Grand Lodge building) was Worshipful Master during that time. The custom during the 1940s and 50s was to bring the entire family to the temple building to enjoy dinner in the large dining hall on the second floor. Down in the basement was an Olympic size swimming pool. After their meal, the men would go upstairs to their lodge meeting, and the wives and children would go down for a swim and visit with friends around the pool. After the meeting, the husbands would come down to join them. Later they may return to the second floor for some coffee or dessert and then go home. It was an enjoyable family event.

This era of Masonic membership prosperity in the U.S. lasted about 20 or 30 years. Then around the 1960s or '70s (depending on the area), a decrease in membership began. The decrease in membership in the U.S. Grand Lodges finally reached a point where Grand Lodges realized that a serious problem was taking place. The income that had been funding the expanded size of the Grand Lodges began to dry up. Older members were dying, and the new members were not coming in at a rate to replace them. On top of this, the remaining members were being suspended for non-payment of dues, demitting out, or just not showing up at lodge. Many lodges began entering a crisis mode.

If you think about it, and if it is correct that there was a desire for entertainment after WWII, then you must think about what else was going on in society around that very time. It is true that for those Masons who desired an enjoyable, family evening out, the lodge provided an excellent means to do it. But all of a sudden, competition for methods of entertainment began. The television was a new entertainment source that began showing up in many homes and, finally, all homes. It was *quickly* accepted by society. The TV was a very convent form of home entertainment. Families could stay at home and be entertained. But then, other new forms of electronic entertainment were created, all designed to provide convenient and fun distraction. For those Masons who saw the lodge as a means of an enjoyable family event, the many new methods of quick and easy amusement were serious competition for Freemasonry.

The problem for Masonry was that it provided nice, wholesome family entertainment, but it was of a limited nature. Once done a few times, the ones seeking only entertainment sought new and better forms. A growing number began preferring staying home and watching TV, or enjoying a nice meal at restaurants, and then a movie. As new forms of electronic entertainment became available, those using Masonry only as a source of entertainment found far better sources outside of the lodge.

When the decrease in memberships began, U.S. Grand Lodges were concerned, and they did not initially understand the reason behind the dramatic loss of membership and participation. Of course, there was also an equal lack of understanding as to why the *increase* in memberships had occurred, which caused the Grand Lodge numbers to swell. But since the increase was a good thing, it seems that not much time was given to understanding it. Grand Lodges needed to find a way first to understand why the numbers were falling and find ways to solve their financial crisis.

By the 1970s and '80s, Grand Lodges began creating various programs designed to bring in new members or try to raise money. *Bring a Friend Night* was a popular program where a lodge would hold some sort of public event or lecture, and the members were encouraged to bring family and non-Masons who may end up being prospective new members. There were also other programs, one of which became known as *One Day, All the Way*. This program was born out of the idea that many prospective candidates were far too busy to wait for sometimes months to go through the three degrees and be subjected to all the time and effort spent to learn the catechisms. So, the idea was to bring a number of lodges together and consolidate all of the candidates in one place (maybe renting a large hall or auditorium). Sometimes several hundred were given all three degrees at one time and in one place in a marathon one-day session. They would forgo all the instruction and memorization for the event. These one-day events seemed popular.

Other bodies liked what they saw and started to piggyback on the Grand Lodges with large Scottish Rite and Shrine events tied to connected weekend *All the Way* programs. A non-Mason could show up on a Friday evening and by Monday morning could be a Master Mason, a 32nd, and maybe even a Shriner.

Almost immediately, questions arose about the validity of these large group initiations. Were the candidates to blame for these events? Were the new members legitimate or *real* Masons. In truth, the questions were never about the reality or validity of the memberships but concern that the abbreviated experience had short-changed the candidates. Deeper looks at the actual nature of initiations began, and many jurisdictions abandoned the practice.

By the late 1970s and early '80s, most Grand Lodges realized that they were in serious trouble. Most of them had started various programs to increase membership (seen as the most viable way to raise money). These programs had varying degrees of success. It was also during this time that two noteworthy events began to take place. These events were completely unrelated to each other and unrelated to the membership efforts of the Grand Lodges. But both of these events turned out to have a substantial impact on the membership situation. One of these events was an anti-

Masonic movement, debatably originating in Texas. The second was a series of books and movies with Freemasonry as the main or secondary subject.

Anti-Masonry has existed for about as long as Freemasonry has existed. Some groups have always felt that Freemasonry was not in keeping with their religious or political beliefs. In Communist states or dictatorships, Freemasonry was stamped out almost immediately. But the seeds for one event which took place in the United States began germinating in the 1980s. A splinter group in the Southern Baptist Convention sought a leadership change in the organization. This group felt that Freemasonry was incompatible with Christianity. It was somewhat ironic that this group would select this topic for their argument as so many in the leadership of the Southern Baptist Convention were, and had been, Freemasons. These events were in the early days of the internet, and this little group took advantage of this new medium for their attacks on both Freemasonry as well as the leadership of the Southern Baptist Convention.

While I will not get deep into this subject, the anti-Masons' arguments were by means of specific charges, which, on the surface, seemed legitimate. Quotes by famous Masons and Grand Lodges were given and cited, which seemed to support their claims. These quotes seemed to suggest that Freemasonry was, indeed, incompatible with Christianity.

The problem for Masonry was that when you looked at the charges being made against Freemasonry as well as the way they were delivered, they seemed logical and were believable. Anyone who knew little to nothing of Masonry could very easily believe these charges. Many did begin believing that there *was* something very wrong with Masonry.

The problem for the anti-Masons was that these charges were false. The charges only gave the *appearance* of being legitimate. What I mean by this is that when the charges were closely examined one by one, sources cited were either out of context, edited to mean something other than the original meaning, or outright created and made up. When honest people examined both the anti-Masonic charges and the answers to the charges by Masons, many felt tricked by the anti-Masons. Christians are not taught to lie or bear false witness. The backlash against the anti-Masons was swift, with many feeling that Freemasonry was being falsely persecuted for commercial means (many of the leading anti-Masons ran companies selling anti-Masonic publications and other propaganda). Many felt that if Freemasonry was of such a nature to have others act so unChristian towards it, then maybe it was of value and worth a closer look. From these anti-Masonic attacks, petitions began coming in from those who found the activities of the anti-Masons not only unChristian but immoral.

Around the same time as the anti-Masonic events were taking place, a completely different and unrelated series of events began. These events can generally be credited to a book that was published in the early 1980s by the title *Holy Blood, Holy Grail*. The book hit like a firestorm and can be seen as touching off a whole era of books and films, all with a Knights Templar/Masonic theme. *Holy Blood, Holy Grail* told the story of the Knights Templar and a secret governing organization. The book told a story of religion and the Church that involved Freemasonry, mystery, and intrigue. It took every element that was necessary for a bestseller and wrapped it together in one package. It was a major bestseller that opened the doors for many similar books and movies. I don't want to suggest that there were no books on Freemasonry or the Templars before this time. Still, this book kicked off a fresh new look at Freemasonry (and related subjects) and resulted in Masonry becoming very popular with the general public. It was this aspect of a romantic and heroic mystery associated with the Templar and Freemasonry that struck a chord with people. Following *Holy Blood, Holy Grail* were books by Dan Brown and a whole series of like books and movies on this "new" (for many) and popular subject.

All these events brought considerable and favorable attention to Freemasonry. And, just like the backlash from the anti-Masonic movement, this new attention brought with it many new petitions by men who had never heard of or thought about joining Freemasonry before this time. These were people who were looking for that *something special.* Based on what they had learned of Freemasonry from these books and films, the Masonic experience was exactly the path they had been seeking.

So, if we step back for a moment, the Grand Lodges were concerned about their falling memberships. They were concerned if their revenue would be enough to meet their needs and had begun programs designed to hopefully increase membership. At the same time, two completely unrelated events were taking place. One was an anti-Masonic movement based on falsehoods about Freemasonry, and the other was a series of popular books and films having Freemasonry as a subject. Both events had the end result of making Freemasonry very attractive to a whole new group of potential members. New members were coming to the doors of lodges not only due to efforts made by the Grand Lodges but also two unforeseen series of events. You would think that these events would put the U.S. Grand Lodges in a very good position. But while the initial results were very positive, many candidates were coming to Freemasonry with preconceived ideas about the lodge experience. Many had read books about Masonry and had certain expectations. In more than a few cases, these expectations were not met.

Let's look at a stereotypical lodge meeting. Realizing that no two lodges are exactly alike, most lodges will meet at about 6 to 7 in the evening. Members will show up a half hour to an hour ahead of time for dinner. It would probably be spaghetti or something similar. After spending a little time visiting with friends and eating dinner, the members will go up to the lodge room. Lodge opens. The Secretary reads the minutes, and the regular business of the lodge is done. The lodge pays bills and reads communications from the Grand Lodge and others. If no degree is taking place, then there may be some discussion of events coming up or repairs or maintenance to the lodge. Then the lodge closes, and maybe they will go downstairs for coffee or a little more talk and then go home. Individuals coming into Masonry expecting an evening of enlightenment or something to enrich their lives would be *very* disappointed. They would know all that they read about Masonry before joining. They would also know that none of what they read had anything at all to do with what they were seeing in the lodge. The actual Masonic experience would be mundane, *at best*. Grand Lodges started reporting a revolving door of members. Men would join but then leave, with some saying they were disappointed. Many times, they would not say anything; they would just walk.

Around this same time, a new development began in a few lodges. It had been brewing for a while but then took off. Some Masons wanted more from the lodge experience. They realized that the stereotypical lodge was not the Masonry they desired or as it once was practiced. What was seen in the lodges was a very minimalistic form of Freemasonry. They wanted something more. They wanted to explore the Masonic symbols, the history, and the ritual. They wanted all the deeper aspects of Masonry incorporated into the lodge experience.

We began to see lodges formed from the desire for something more, calling themselves "traditional observance" lodges. Members of these lodges would regularly meet in tuxedos or, at least, business suits to give a more formal air to the lodge setting. Minutes of the prior meeting were printed and left on tables to be read by any interested to give the lodge more time for the delivery of educational papers. All regular business of the lodge was conducted at officer business meetings so that the reading of the electric bill, rent, and so on would not cut into the valuable time that could be spent on education. Every lodge meeting was considered an event, and they would try to make the very most out of every gathering. These lodges met in stark contrast to the stereotypical lodges, and they began a feeling that this was true Freemasonry. The stereotypical lodge was something other than a Masonic lodge. A division was created.

It is this division between the two styles of lodges that I have considered. My thought is that Freemasonry is of such a nature that we all seek our own level in it. My own desired personal lodge experience is one that is more enlightening rather than just dinner and a business meeting. I enjoy learning something and leaving the lodge with a deeper understanding of Freemasonry than when I walked in the door. But, I realize that I do not speak for everyone. I realize that while my desire should not be denied, my desire should also not be imposed on others. I've recognized for many years that there are many Masons who simply enjoy going to lodge to enjoy a meal and a little conversation with their friends. These are honest, sincere men who would give you the shirt off their back to help you. They are deeply worthy, but they just do not have the same goals in Masonry as the goals of others. So what?

These divisions in the lodges soon began to create disharmony as there was the suggestion that one or the other was not valid Masonry. I find these attitudes disappointing. I believe that a lodge should reflect the attitude and desires of the members. If someone is a member of a lodge and that lodge is not meeting their needs or requirements, that does not mean that the lodge is bad or not *real* Masonry. It only means that the lodge and the member are not a proper fit. This is where I believe that Freemasons should exercise their own good common sense and reasoning abilities. If we realize that we are in a lodge that is not a good fit for us, then we should join one that *is* a good fit. If we cannot find a lodge that is a good fit, then we should try and find those of like mind and create a lodge. By doing this, we can satisfy our needs but not tear down the needs of anyone else.

The goal of Freemasonry is the same as it has always been. It is to take those who are basically good and then give them the tools, lessons, and symbolic teachings, to help them improve themselves. The way that we work as a lodge depends on what we seek out of Freemasonry. If our goals lead us in one direction, we must realize that the goals of others may lead them in different directions. The Masonic lodge experience can be looked at as a music experience. If you go to a music concert and happen to enjoy country and western music, this may not appeal to someone who enjoys blues. Another person may prefer an opera. None of these are better than the other. They are just different styles of music. The same is true of Freemasonry. Don't be confused by the many changes going on. They do not mean bad things. Many now see their lodge experience as a more formal event designed to teach the deeper aspects of Masonry. There are certain formats for these lodges. There are many young and old Masons who desire this style of lodge.

On the other hand, many Masons simply enjoy the company of their brothers and seek only the fellowship that the lodge offers. Very little is expected in these lodges. No one should see this as one style being better than the other. It is simply different preferences. The only problem that can come is if one style of Freemasonry attempts to judge the other. In such cases, then it is a sign that more basic Masonic education is needed.

In a world of change, we balance change with our own common sense. We should not be forced into unwanted, unnecessary changes, nor should we be forced to refrain from taking part in desired change. Freemasonry should be a tool for personal growth, not a weight around our neck.

What is Esoterism?

When the student is ready, the master appears.
~ Buddhist Proverb

Can you imagine somehow going back in time to the Middle Ages, standing in a crowd of people, and then receiving a call on your cell phone? How do you believe the people around you would react? Humans evaluate and respond to situations based on their experiences. We all have heard cell phones ring and someone answering a call. We may not know exactly how the thing works, but we have experience with cell phones and recognize them as a common communication device. But how would someone in the Middle Ages, with their life experiences, view such an event? Would we be seen as some sort of magician who was using, maybe, evil powers? Most likely. Would we generate fear in those around us and be in some physical danger? Most probably. Cell phones did not exist in the Middle Ages. Nothing like them existed. They would have been viewed as something beyond reason and impossible to exist within the normal manner of life. It would be a *magical* device. At that time in history, whatever was viewed as existing beyond the realm of everyday life was the unknown, the esoteric, the dangerous, the magical … the evil. It was the only way such things could be explained.

Claude Bernard tells us: "Man can learn nothing except by going from the known to the unknown." Even when we consider the powerful fear of the unknown, our human quest for knowledge has always existed and was never, for long, denied. We were and are curious beings. In the early days of mankind, lightning striking a tree must have been a terrifying event, and the tree must have been viewed as dangerous long after the strike. But this would not have stopped a curious few from approaching and touching the "dangerous" tree. Maybe they could not properly explain why they did such a foolish thing, but they simply *had* to do it. They *had* to reach out.

The end of the Dark Ages was an ignorant, violent, and fearful time. If you did something to create fear in another, you would most likely face harm — and fear of magic or the unknown and unexplainable was a profound fear. The dawn of the Middle Ages saw the Church as the accepted source of all legitimate information, knowledge, and answers. To seek answers for what was not explained or beyond what was given by the Church would put your very life in danger. Yet there were those who did just that. They questioned information or answers given by the Church. They sought to learn for themselves and reach beyond the limited teachings of the Church. They knowingly sought knowledge at the risk of their lives. They simply *had* to do it. They *had* to reach out. These seekers of Light gave birth to what we know today as esoterism, but really, also medicine, science, and a host of other fields. In the words of Albert Einstein, "The most beautiful thing we can experience is the mystical. It is the source of all true art and science."

Esoteric knowledge or teachings were the private or inner teachings that were never made available to everyone. In most all cases, these teachings were carefully guarded as to be associated with them could be an actual death sentence. Small groups of students would gather to explore all aspects of themselves and the world around them in total secrecy. Vows and oaths were often required of new members in order to protect them and to better the chance of the continuation of the group.

It was in this atmosphere that the seeds of what we have today as Freemasonry were sown. How old is Freemasonry? Before you can begin to answer that question, you must answer, "What is Freemasonry?" In his classic "The Secret Teachings of All Ages," Manly P. Hall writes:

"The sanctum sanctorum of Freemasonry is ornamented with the gnostic jewels of a thousand ages; its rituals ring with the divinely inspired words of seers and sages. A hundred religious have brought their gifts of wisdom to its altar; arts and sciences unnumbered have contributed to its symbolism. Freemasonry is a world-wide university teaching the liberal arts and sciences of the soul to all who will hearken to its words. Its chairs are seats of learning, and its pillars uphold an arch of universal education. Its trestleboards are inscribed with the eternal verities of all ages and upon those who comprehend its sacred depths has dawned the realization that within the Freemasonic Mysteries lie hidden the long-lost arcana sought by all peoples since the genesis of human reason.

17

"The philosophic power of Freemasonry lies in its symbols — its priceless heritage from the Mystery schools of antiquity. In a letter to Robert Freke Gould, Albert Pike writes:

'It began to shape itself to my intellectual vision into something more imposing and majestic, solemnly mysterious and grand. It seemed to me like the Pyramids in their loneliness, in whose yet undiscovered chambers may be hidden, for the enlightenment of coming generations, the sacred books of the Egyptians, so long lost to the world; like the Sphynx half buried in the desert. In its symbolism, which and its spirit of brotherhood are its essence, Freemasonry is more ancient than any of the world's living religions. It has the symbols and doctrines which, older than himself, Zarathustra inculcated; and seemed to me a spectacle sublime, yet pitiful — the ancient Faith of our ancestors holding out to the world its symbols once so eloquent, and mutely and in vain asking for an interpreter. And so I came at last to see that the true greatness and majesty of Freemasonry consist in its proprietorship of these and its other symbols; and that its symbolism is its soul.'

"Though the temples of Thebes and Karnak be now but majestic heaps of broken and time-battered stone, the spirit: of Egyptian philosophy still marches triumphant through the centuries. Though the rock-hewn sanctuaries of the ancient Brahmins be now deserted, and their carvings crumbled into dust, still the wisdom of the Vedas endures. Though the oracles be silenced, and the House of the Mysteries be now but rows of ghostly columns, still shines the spiritual glory of Hellas with luster undiminished. Though Zoroaster, Hermes, Pythagoras, Plato, and Aristotle are now but dim memories in a world once rocked by the transcendency of their intellectual genius, still in the mystic temple of Freemasonry these god-men live again in their words and symbols; and the candidate, passing through the initiations, feels himself face to face with these illumined hierophants of days long past."[1]

When the little groups of knowledge seekers illegally gathered, they could not speak or teach freely. They could not, even within their own group, provide open educational material for fear that it would be discovered, resulting in imprisonment or death for all. So, they employed the use of symbols to teach. It was not a new way of teaching. Teaching by symbols has been in use since the dawn of mankind. But it was effective. Profound teachings could be presented by the use of symbols, and those uneducated in the meaning of the symbols would be able to see nothing of what was being taught. It was not only an effective way to teach, but it provided security.

Freemasonry teaches by using symbols because its roots are in the very esoteric groups that used this method to teach. Esoterism is not a foreign subject to Freemasonry but is as much a part of the fabric of Freemasonry as is initiation.

NOTES:

1. Manly P. Hall, *The Secret Teachings of All Ages* (Los Angeles: The Philosophical Research Society, 1977 reprint), p. 176 [CLXXVI].

Who is more foolish, the child afraid of the dark or the man afraid of the light?

~ Maurice Freehill

Masonic Alchemy

The greatest discovery of my generation is that a human being can
alter his life by altering his attitudes.

~ William James

When we speak of alchemy and Freemasonry together, it can be a flashpoint for argument. Masons sometimes view alchemy, especially when connected to Freemasonry, as something akin to *booga booga* nonsense. Alchemists are often viewed as nutty old men in long robes doing strange things, all with the goal of swindling ignorant medieval royalty out of their wealth. Alchemists are seen by some as opportunistic con-men who played on the ignorance, superstition, and greed of their victims.

Of alchemy and the old alchemists, Manly P. Hall writes in his classic "The Secret Teachings of all Ages":

"Is the transmutation of base metals into gold possible? Is the idea one at which the learned of the modern world can afford to scoff? Alchemy was more than a speculative art: it was also an operative art. Since the time of the immortal Hermes, alchemists have asserted (and not without substantiating evidence) that they could manufacture gold from tin, silver, lead, and mercury. That the galaxy of brilliant philosophic and scientific minds who, over a period of two thousand years, affirmed the actuality of metallic transmutation and multiplication, could be completely sane and rational on all other problems of philosophy and science, yet hopelessly mistaken on this one point, is untenable. Nor is it reasonable that the hundreds declaring to have seen and performed transmutations of metals could all have been dupes, imbeciles, or liars.

"Those assuming that all alchemists were of unsound mentality would be forced to put in this category nearly all the philosophers and scientists of the ancient and medieval worlds. Emperors, princes, priests, and common townsfolk have witnessed the apparent miracle of metallic metamorphosis. In the face of existing testimony, anyone is privileged to remain unconvinced, but the scoffer elects to ignore evidence worthy of respectful consideration. Many great alchemists and Hermetic philosophers occupy an honored niche in the Hall of Fame, while their multitudinous critics remain obscure. To list all these sincere seekers after Nature's great arcanum is impossible, but a few will suffice to acquaint the reader with the superior types of intellect who interested themselves in this abstruse subject.

"Among the more prominent names are those of Thomas Norton, Isaac of Holland, Basil Valentine (the supposed discoverer of antimony), Jean de

Meung, Roger Bacon, Albertus Magnus, Gerber (the Arabian who brought the knowledge of alchemy to Europe through his writings), Paracelsus, Nicholas Flamel, John Frederick Helvetius, Raymond Lully, Alexander Seton, Michael Sendivogius, Count Bernard of Treviso, Sir George Ripley, Pico della Mirandola, John Dee, Henry Khunrath, Michael Maier, Thomas Vaughan, J. B. van Helmont, John Heydon, Lascaris, Thomas Charnock, Synesius (Bishop of Ptolemais), Morieu, the Comte di Cagliostro, and the Comte de St.-Germain. There are legends to the effect that King Solomon and Pythagoras were alchemists and that the former manufactured by alchemical means the gold used in his temple.

"Albert Pike takes sides with the alchemical philosophers by declaring that the gold of the Hermetists was a reality. He says: "The Hermetic science, like all the real sciences, is mathematically demonstrable. Its results, even material, are as rigorous as that of a correct equation. The Hermetic Gold is not only a true dogma, a light without Shadow, a Truth without alloy of falsehood; it is also a material gold, real, pure, the most precious that can be found in the mines of the earth."[1]

My father was a career military man who retired as a full Colonel from the Army. I grew up living on an Army base and actually joined Freemasonry still living on that base. When my father retired, he wanted to do something that he enjoyed, made him feel creative, and relaxed him. He did something unexpected; he became a jeweler. He enjoyed creating pieces of jewelry. One day I was talking with my dad (a Freemason and Rosicrucian) about alchemy. He started laughing and asked, "When a jeweler creates a new piece of gold jewelry, do you *really* think that they use a piece of real gold to work on and take the chance of destroying something that expensive?" He pointed out that artificial gold is always used to practice on as the cost is far, far less, and the look and feel are just like real gold. He also noted that just like artificial gold exists, so do artificial gems, which are "grown" and even sold as such — one of the most popular being cubic zirconia which has the look and feel of genuine diamonds. It's not "*booga booga* nonsense;" it's what is common practice all over the world and is a large part of the jewelry business. It is also a fact that if a piece of artificial gold or an artificial gem were put in your hand, most people would have no idea that it was anything but real. In many cases, it would take a trained jeweler with expensive, modern equipment to analyze and ascertain the real from the fake. So, if the old alchemists created the same "fake gold" how could anyone (including the old alchemists) know or tell if it was *real* gold or not?

Is it possible to make *real* gold from base metal? I've never done it. But it is possible to make something that *looks*, *feels*, and *seems* like real gold. It's done all the time. So, if you were to go back in time to when the alchemists were the "nutty old men in long robes" and they handed you (or some king) something that looked like, felt like, and by every known standard of the time *was* gold, what would be the conclusion? So again, is alchemy real?

But was the reserved goal of alchemy ever to simply change base metals into gold? Could there be something more? Alchemy brings about a perceived change. It claims to take something less and make it of greater value. What does Freemasonry do? Do we claim to take good men and make them better? Is that a change and an improvement? Isn't that alchemy?

The alchemical process is a complex series of events with the goal of improving the nature of something — making it of more value. A moral, upright, and educated man is viewed as of more value to society than a rogue. Freemasonry was initially designed to be a complex series of events (initiations and teachings) with the goal of taking someone basically good and helping them to become a better human being. The degrees of Freemasonry can be viewed as the alchemical steps. By comparing the rituals of any Masonic rite and looking at the various old alchemical texts, we can see very similar core steps or instructions. We can see that it is very reasonable that one "borrowed" from the other. The concepts and fundamental goals of both alchemy and Freemasonry are too similar to discount some association and basic connection in the formative time of our Craft.

In the Star Wars movie, "The Empire Strikes Back," the young Jedi, Luke, unsuccessfully attempted to lift his X-wing fighter from a swamp. After several attempts, he gave up. He told the Jedi Master, Yoda, that lifting the fighter was impossible with the force as Yoda asked him to do. Before lifting the X-wing out of the swamp himself, Yoda told Luke: "You must unlearn what you have learned." There is profound wisdom in that statement. There are times when many of us hold onto ideas, concepts, or beliefs that deny us the opportunity of living a fuller, richer life.

As a boy, a good friend of mine had an older brother who was the source of all good information for us. He was older and far more experienced than the rest of us. We would be foolish not to listen to him. One day, I remember going to an ice cream shop with my friend, his older brother, and a few others. One of us started to order strawberry ice cream. The older boy jumped in saying that strawberry was the *worst* flavor made. He said that he would *never* eat it, and anyone who did would be doing so at their own risk. Well, that was enough for me. I never touched the stuff until I was an adult. Even then, it was only because I was in an awkward situation. I was invited over to a friend's house for dinner. After dinner, his wife brought in the dessert — homemade strawberry ice cream. I was uneasy as I knew it would taste horrible, but I *had* to eat it or risk insulting them. To my amazement, it was wonderful! All through my childhood and for years into my adulthood, I denied myself something very good because I accepted something untested as a fact. I had to "unlearn" what I had learned about strawberry ice cream. What I also learned later was that there was a reason this older boy had such feelings about this flavor of ice cream. It turns out that he had a severe allergy to strawberries. It was not that he disliked the taste, but that strawberries did bad things to him.

Luke was his own worst enemy because of his early teachings. I was my own worst enemy because of what I believed. We all need to evaluate what we know as "fact" and explore the possibilities that new truths might await us when we open up to them. Freemasonry may be more than a club. Our rituals may be more than just moral plays. And alchemy may be something we wish to explore a little deeper.

NOTES:

1. Manly P. Hall, *The Secret Teachings of All Ages* (Los Angeles: The Philosophical Research Society, 1977 reprint), p. 149 [CXLIX].

Do or do not. There is no try.

~ Yoda

Freemasons and Rosicrucians

Of all the theories which have been advanced in relation to the origin of Freemasonry from some one of the secret sects, either of antiquity or of the Middle Ages, there is none more interesting than that which seeks to connect it with the Hermetic philosophy, because there is none which presents more plausible claims to our consideration.

~ Albert G. Mackey

There is a thought that either one has always been a Rosicrucian, or they never will be one. I believe the same is true of Freemasonry. But what does that mean? We are told that we are first made a Mason in our heart. What can that mean?

Some believe that who we are in the deepest reaches of our heart (soul, spirit, being) defines us and has always been of that nature, unchanged. With that, the deepest qualities of what it means to be a Freemason, or a Rosicrucian, have always been with us (or not), and membership only affords us the opportunity to explore the organizational philosophy in a setting, maybe, better suited for our personal advancement. I happen to be one who shares such a belief.

My dog responds to her name. I can speak many other words, but there is no reaction in her. When I say her name, she responds. If I spoke my dog's name to another dog, there would probably be no response. There is nothing wrong with a dog that did not respond to my dog's name any more than there is anything wrong with my dog for not responding to another dog's name. All respond to what is familiar to them. There is nothing wrong with a philosophy reaching deep into one person, yet not another. We all have different paths. A problem can come, however, if we pretend that something is reached by us when it is not. This can lead to changing what we do not understand into something we may *think* is understandable. Mistakes can then happen. If you do not understand the use of a pen and drive it into a wall like a nail, then you have denied yourself the proper use and benefit of a pen. For you, its use has changed and became limited, and, not even as effective as a nail. An even greater danger than not knowing something is when it is coupled with the arrogant assumption that we "know it all."

I also happen to believe that, for me, there is a deep connection and tie between Rosicrucianism and Freemasonry. The connection is through the various initiations.

In his "Rosicrucian and Masonic Origins," Manly P. Hall writes:

> "Freemasonry is a fraternity within a fraternity — an outer organization concealing an inner brotherhood of the elect. Before it is possible to intelligently discuss the origin of the Craft, it is necessary, therefore, to establish the existence of these two separate yet interdependent orders, the one

visible and the other invisible. The visible society is a splendid camaraderie of "free and accepted" men enjoined to devote themselves to ethical, educational, fraternal, patriotic, and humanitarian concerns. The invisible society is a secret and most august fraternity whose members are dedicated to the service of a mysterious arcanum arcanorum. Those Brethren who have essayed to write the history of their Craft have not included in their disquisitions the story of that truly secret inner society which is to the body Freemasonic what the heart is to the body human. In each generation only a few are accepted into the inner sanctuary of the Work, but these are veritable Princes of the Truth, and their sainted names shall be remembered in future ages together with the seers and prophets of the elder world. Though the great initiate-philosophers of Freemasonry can be counted upon one's fingers, yet their power is not to be measured by the achievements of ordinary men. They are dwellers upon the Threshold of the Innermost, Masters of that secret doctrine which forms the invisible foundation of every great theological and rational institution."

Why do we have initiations? Do we employ them for the benefit of the members watching the "plays," or do they have a deeper importance for the candidates?

There is a thought that for an initiation (Masonic, Rosicrucian, or any other) to be of true value to the candidate, there must be the proper setting, a desire to initiate, and a desire to be initiated. A lack in any of these elements may result in a failed initiation. The words and floorwork may be correct, and the initiation completely "legal" in the eyes of the Grand Lodge, but that special *something* that sometimes touches a candidate deep within may be missing. That *something* is what sets us apart from clubs and worthy charitable associations. It's what makes us kindred to the Ancient Mystery Schools and associates us with other mystical orders.

Proper initiation is thought to open *doors* for us. We may think of this in the physical sense and think of an actual door opening up and allowing us entrance into another room of a building. We may also think of this *building* as something much larger and not physical. The *door* that leads us to this other room may be thought of as the initiation itself.

A proper initiation assists us in traveling from one level (*room*) to another, to bring us to places and afford us the opportunity for continued development or enlightenment. In all cases, it is our choice to accept and travel on, reject and remain in place, or return to where we were. Each travels their own path. Each develops as they are guided. One path may be wholly unsuitable for one while a perfect fit for another. We should try to refrain from judgments regarding path choices. Zen philosophy teaches, "No snowflake ever falls in the wrong place." It's not our place to judge the path of others.

The Rosicrucians are a *room* that a *door* may open for us. It is a path on the continuing journey towards self-development. It is a mistake to believe that Rosicrucianism (any more than Freemasonry) is a social club or a reward to be bestowed on those deemed popular, worthy, or useful. You cannot give something to one who already has it or will never have it. You cannot *become* a Rosicrucian, nor have it taken away from you. You can only associate with others of like mind.

A proper initiation may make you aware of who and what you are. The opening of a door may allow you to feel things long forgotten, or it may only take you to an empty place of no use to you. We are who we are, and it is only by expanding ourselves do we learn our path.

The Rosicrucians are tied to Freemasons just as one road leads to another in a long journey. Even if we all end our journey at the same destination, there is no requirement for all to travel on the same path. For some Rosicrucians and some Freemasons, the path is too similar to ignore, and they recognize the mystic tie. Being a Rosicrucian is, for some, the same in their deepest being as is being a Freemason. But this path may have no meaning whatsoever to another. There is no gain in one path or loss in another.

Also, in "Rosicrucian and Masonic Origins," Manly Hall writes:

"A new day is dawning for Freemasonry. From the insufficiency of theology and the hopelessness of materialism, men are turning to seek the God of philosophy. In this new era wherein the old order of things is breaking down and the individual is rising triumphant above the monotony of the masses, there is much work to be accomplished. The "Temple Builder" is needed as never before. A great reconstruction period is at hand; the debris of a fallen culture must be cleared away; the old footings must be found again that a new Temple significant of a new revelation of Law may be raised thereon. This is the peculiar work of the Builder; this is the high duty for which he was called out of the world; this is the noble enterprise for which he was "raised" and given the tools of his Craft. By thus doing his part in the reorganization of society, the workman may earn his "wages" as all good Masons should. A new light is breaking in the East, a more glorious day is at hand. The rule of the philosophic elect-the dream of the ages-will yet be realized and is not far distant. To her loyal sons, Freemasonry sends this clarion call: "Arise ye, the day of labor is at band; the Great Work awaits completion, and the days of man's life are few." Like the singing guildsman of bygone days, the Craft of the Builders marches victoriously down the broad avenues of Time. Their song is of labor and glorious endeavor; their anthem is of toil and industry; they rejoice in their noble destiny, for they are the Builders of cities, the Hewers of worlds, the Master Craftsmen of the universe!"

We have work to do. Let's find our path and travel it.

Who looks outside, dreams; who looks inside, awakes.

~ Carl Gustav Jung

Forgiveness and Freemasonry

Forgiveness has nothing to do with absolving a criminal of his crime. It has everything to do with relieving oneself of the burden of being a victim — letting go of the pain and transforming oneself from victim to survivor.

~ C.R. Strahan

The act of forgiving is a cornerstone tenet of most religions. Christianity is built around the concept of the Grand Architect forgiving the sins of the deserving. Likewise, Freemasonry teaches the concept of seeking forgiveness in its most basic teachings. In the closing prayer of lodges, forgiveness is sought from the Almighty: "Pardon, we beseech Thee, whatever Thou hast seen amiss in us ..." (*Louisiana Masonic Monitor* p.15). We are taught that humans are far from perfect creatures, and if we could not seek redemption for our transgressions, then our lives could be seen as hopeless.

We are also taught that forgiveness is not only something that should be *sought* but that we should *extend* forgiveness to those who have wronged us. "And when you stand praying, if you hold anything against anyone, forgive

35

him, so that your Father in heaven may forgive you your sins." (Mark 11:25)

The extending of forgiveness to another human is sometimes, however, a point of confusion. Why are we forgiving this person? What is the benefit of forgiving another? What conditions must exist before we can extend forgiveness? What is expected after we forgive someone?

If we cannot clearly understand why we are forgiving someone, or what it means to forgive, then it would seem to be a pointless and empty act. One concept is that when we forgive someone, the one being forgiven is the one who benefits. This belief, however, does not provide satisfactory answers to all questions. What if the one being forgiven does not seek or care about forgiveness? In addition, the sometimes spoken, and sometimes implied, condition for forgiveness is that the offense is not repeated. Do repeated offenses or refusal to request forgiveness give cause for it to be withheld?

In Freemasonry, we are taught that the Bible is to be the rule and guide to our faith and practices. If this is so, then the Bible does not always seem to require that forgiveness be sought by our fellow man. In Matthew 18:21-22, the Bible simply tells us to forgive others (and to do so as often as needed). "Then Peter came to Jesus and asked, 'Lord, how many times shall I forgive my brother when he sins against me? Up to seven times?' Jesus answered, 'I tell you, not seven times, but seventy-seven times.' "

If forgiving the one who causes the offense is to be extended even if it is not requested/wanted and even if the same offense occurs repeatedly, then does this mean that the Bible is telling us to be rather foolish? Does it mean there are no consequences for our actions, and one should be rewarded for bad behavior? I do not believe so.

The perceived problem may come from our associating and linking forgiveness with consequences. Forgiveness is relational. Consequences are circumstantial. If, during an angry argument, we were to take the treasured antique vase of a loved one and throw it to the ground, breaking it into tiny pieces, what would happen next? Well, that depends on the parties involved. If we sincerely apologize for our actions, it is possible that our loved one will forgive us, and we can move on from the event. But nothing we can ever do will erase the fact that the vase was destroyed. That's done and is a consequence of our actions. It can't be undone.

In the Bible, Paul wrote, "Do not be deceived: God cannot be mocked. People reap what they sow." (Gal. 6:7). Forgiveness for our actions does not mean that there are no consequences for those actions.

Let's take Freemasonry and try to apply this thought. Let's say that your lodge has a family night where Masons and non-Masons are enjoying a very nice dinner in your lodge hall. A well-liked member of the lodge comes into the hall obviously drunk. He soon begins to cause disturbances. Someone mentions his condition to him, and this only outrages him. He begins throwing over tables and creates a major disturbance. This alone is grounds for a Masonic trial. Masons do not act this way. But Masons are also taught to help each other and lift up a fallen brother. Let's say that a few days after the event, the member contacts the lodge officers and gives a heartfelt apology for what happened. He explains that some unfortunate personal events in his life caused him to break in such a manner. The officers cannot point to any like event by this brother in the past and believe that he is truly sorry for his actions. They deliberate. After some thought and consideration of the events, Masonic charity comes into play. They do not file Masonic charges on him and only advise him to take better control of his life.

Did the lodge officers act improperly by not insisting that he face trial? I don't believe so. They fully realized that this was a very serious situation. They weighed all aspects of what happened and what they should do. This was not something that the brother had done before, it was unlike him, he expressed sincere regret, and gave assurance that it would not happen again. As humans, we all fail from time to time. I believe that nothing more could be done and that they acted responsibly for the good of the Order. They forgave him.

Now, let's go forward a bit in time. It's now the end of the year, the brother who caused the disturbance has not again shown up at lodge drunk, and has caused no further disturbances. The lodge has a large family event for presenting awards to various members. The brother who caused the drunken disturbance is named "Mason of the Year" and given a beautiful plaque. He is then called up before the lodge for pictures with the Worshipful Master. All because he did not show up drunk again. What is the message?

When we deal with consequences, there is no right or wrong, no moral or immoral; there is only cause and effect. What we might want, or desire, does not offset the consequence resulting from an event.

Whatever the intention of the Worshipful Master in giving this brother this award (even if he feels it is a noble reason), this selection could objectively be seen as inappropriate based on what happened earlier in the year. The reasonable result is to portray Freemasonry as a group that rewards (or does not care about) bad behavior. This is the message sent and received no matter what the Worshipful Master or lodge desired or intended. It is the consequence of selecting this particular member, with his previous actions, for this award. And, with it, the reputation of Freemasonry may be permanently damaged for all who know of only the drunken display.

The lodge officers honored their obligation to who they believed to be a deserving brother, but they were also obligated to protect the reputation of our Order. They should have looked more objectively at the *entire* picture and selected another deserving brother for this award. Both the drunken member and the lodge officers failed in different ways, and both actions resulted in consequences. Good judgment does not seem to have been used in either case.

And what of the predicament when we are told that we must forgive, but the offender does not seek forgiveness or continues with his objectionable behavior? Unconditional forgiveness can be seen as an affront against justice and a denial of the significance of the wrongdoing and its damaging effects. The Bible even presents us with what could be viewed as a contradictory message from the ones given earlier: "If your brother or sister sins against you, rebuke them; and if they repent, forgive them. Even if they sin against you seven times in a day and seven times come back to you saying, 'I repent,' you must forgive them." (Luke 17:3-4) Notice how the act of forgiveness is qualified ("if they repent"). If they don't repent, the suggestion is that they should not be forgiven.

This goes to the question of *why* we should forgive and what *is* forgiveness. Forgiveness can be seen as a pardon for offenses or a release of negative feelings, depending on how the act of forgiveness is used. In both cases, forgiveness is a choice. The consequence is not a choice, but the result of an action. If someone accidentally bumps into you in a store, the polite thing for them to do is apologize. The event is usually soon forgotten, and the act's consequences are so minor that they are also soon forgotten. If one is rude enough to bump into you and walk away with no apology or even arrogance over the event, the memory of the event may remain longer. However, since it is still minor, it will pass away before very long. Serious acts, however, may never be forgotten and can change (or completely destroy) the nature of even close relationships.

In truth, we should not forgive for the benefit of others, but for our own benefit. It is understood that sometimes a person does not intend to change his behavior. He may not care about what anyone thinks of his actions. We don't forgive him for his sake but because having anger, hurt, and upset within us does not help us in any manner. Negative feelings tear us down and prevent us from doing the good we should be doing. We are not pardoning an act, but letting it go so that it does not drag us down. We have no ability to change another, but we have total control over what we think and how we act. We *can* change our outlook. We *can* choose to let go of feelings that can lead to bitterness. It does not mean that there are no consequences for actions. There may be no pardon for the act, and relationships may be forever destroyed because of it, but you do not have to carry anger within you. This *is* a form of forgiveness. It means only that we wish to live in peace and choose to let go of the pain.

In Masonry, we are taught that if we have a serious issue with another Mason, we should try to work out the problem. If we cannot, we should not risk the peace and harmony of the lodge. We should withdraw from a meeting rather than allow the lodge to suffer. There is a message here. We *can* forgive someone and have peace in our heart. But because of past actions, we might not have a close relationship (or any at all) with someone who has wronged us. We can walk away from the "meeting" for the sake of peace and harmony. We are in control of our own feelings and actions.

Resentment is like drinking poison and then hoping it will kill your enemies.

~ Nelson Mandela

Maundy Thursday in the Scottish Rite

*The purpose of life is not to be happy. It is to be useful, to be
honorable, to be compassionate, to have it make some difference
that you have lived and lived well.*
~ Ralph Waldo Emerson

Maundy Thursday is recognized in most of the world
as one of the Christian Holy Days, specifically the Thursday
before Easter Sunday. This is remembered by the Last Supper
with Jesus and the Apostles. Maundy Thursday also plays a
role and has significance to the Scottish Rite mainly through
the Chapter Rose Croix. The Maundy Thursday ceremony
was used for many years in remembrance of this day in many
Scottish Rite valleys. This was an obligatory ceremony in the
Southern Jurisdiction from the 1870s until about 1994. All
Rose Croix chapters would have a Maundy Thursday
ceremony with the memberships in attendance – or absent
with excuse. This ceremony is today officially renamed the
Remembrance Ceremony and is no longer obligatory.

The oldest known printed ceremony of the Maundy
Thursday ceremony is from 1856 and was published by
Charles Laffon de Ladebat. De Ladebat was a Sovereign
Grand Inspector General of the Supreme Council of Louisiana

in New Orleans. At the time of the Concordat of 1855 between the Supreme Council of Louisiana and the Supreme Council SJ USA, de Ladebat affiliated with the Southern Jurisdiction and became one of their Sovereign Grand Inspectors General. He is also known as one of the principal Scottish Rite instructors of the young Albert Pike.

The Maundy Thursday ceremony was most likely an older New Orleans Scottish Rite ceremony that de Ladebat had in his possession from the Supreme Council of Louisiana, but we have no records to confirm this theory. As the ceremony is no longer worked by the Southern Jurisdiction, those wishing to see a copy of it might check with their Valley Secretary to see if copies are still available. The beautiful ceremony teaches charity and brotherhood. It is no longer worked by the SJ as apparently some felt that it was too Christian or religious in nature. I imagine the concern was that some might view it as elevating one faith above others.

Because of the nature of words and their meanings, there is sometimes confusion in how we define "religion" and "religious." There seems to be the thought that if something is *religious*, then it must be part of a specific *religion*. I don't believe this to be necessarily true. But it does seem that when something is done in the name of religion, some apply it directly to a particular religious faith or branch of that faith.

The fallacy of the above thought can be illustrated if we look at a Roman Catholic priest. If during a Mass, the priest says: "Be good. Do what is right. Don't hurt others. Be honorable. Be fair." Does that mean that anyone who is not a Roman Catholic should discount what the priest says out of concern that they do not wish to seem to be Roman Catholic?

The fact is that there are universal truths that are shared by all sincere religions. No one faith has the monopoly on being good and helping others. Freemasonry has always used ceremonies from various religions that are meaningful to its quest for self-improvement. Yes, the Maundy Thursday ceremony is based on a Christian ceremony, and if you think about it, it makes perfect sense. The ceremony was used in Rose-Croix chapters. A Rose-Croix Knight is a very thinly veiled Knight Templar. It is one of the Templar degrees in the Scottish Rite, and the Knights Templar were Christian.

The fact that the Scottish Rite uses this Christian ceremony does not mean that it is advancing one faith above others. As an example, I'll use myself. To the best of my knowledge, I have no Italian blood in me. Regardless, I still very much enjoy Italian food. I enjoy Chinese food. My liking something that is associated with another group of people does not mean that I am denying who I am or trying to be something that I am not. It only means that I can appreciate things that are not associated with me or part of my own culture and heritage. Freemasonry takes moral lessons from a number of faiths.

The Maundy Thursday ceremony centered mainly on the concept of giving and sharing, of helping to provide for those in need. In Christianity, the ceremony is representative of the Last Supper. But the idea of breaking bread or sharing a meal with others has symbolic connotations far earlier than Christianity. There has always been a need for humans to be social. The idea of sharing food with others is natural and instinctual within us all. The need to be associated with others is a fundamental part of us. Eating and sharing food fulfills this internal requisite. This is what is taught and offered in the Maundy Thursday ceremony that the Scottish Rite used.

When you look at the surface of a ceremony, you may see something that is beautiful. But, by looking deeper, you can find the hidden gems. This is especially true of ceremonies of the Scottish Rite. The Maundy Thursday ceremony is not simply about sharing but teaching us to build on all we have already learned in the craft lodge. If we have paid attention, it is the end result of our learning. If we look at the Scottish Rite craft degrees, we learn of the lesson of Hiram (just like the craft degrees of all rites), but in the Scottish Rite craft degrees, the story is told a bit different. In the lesson of Hiram, we learn of three "bad guys." In the Scottish Rite craft ceremony, we are taught that these "bad guys" represent three specific human failures: ignorance, falsehood, and ambition. Now, think about the charitable acts that are taking place in the Maundy Thursday ceremony. If one were to give in to any of these human failings, we should not expect him to understand or participate in advanced acts of human enlightenment. Ignorance, falsehood, and ambition can be seen as the root causes of most of the problems in the world. Sharing, giving, and being charitable are far less possible if one has fallen to one of these flaws.

If one is ignorant, then they don't know the right thing to do. Falsehood is often born out of ignorance. Someone may be ignorant of the truth, so they will accept something false. And the greatest killer of all is ambition. Those seeking only power, glory, and fame will often be the ones found at the heart of most of the problems we face.

We cannot serve two masters at the same time. There is no room in our hearts for the failings of the "bad guys" as well as the beauty of the teachings within the Maundy Thursday ceremony. It is why the ceremony was for so many years obligatory. But, even then, we are taught that those who could not attend should take a few moments out of their day and spend a little time in private thought. The idea was to think about what is truly important in life, what is important for the growth of our spirit. The goal is to learn and then to teach; to grow and then to help others to grow; to gain and then share. This is represented by taking a small amount of bread and eating it, then passing it to another. It is a simple, beautiful, and deeply profound ceremony.

Even though the Scottish Rite no longer requires this ceremony, it can be of great value to all who are of a like mind. If those of the same desire gather, even in their own homes, on a certain schedule for a little time of private, spiritual "sharing" of peace, kindness, and giving. It can be a beneficial and rewarding time. By doing this, a bond can be created between those of like spirit.

We can help, and should help, each other grow and improve. I believe that this is the meaning of the Maundy Thursday ceremony. It is something we should keep alive in our hearts.

You have not lived today until you have done something for someone who can never repay you.

~ John Bunyan

The *Highest* Masonic Degree
(Human Ego)

Be yourself; everyone else is already taken.
~ Oscar Wilde

A young Mason asked: "If the Master Mason degree is the highest degree that can be attained in Masonry, why do the Scottish Rite and York Rite say they have degrees which are higher?" This is an often-asked and logical question from more than a few Masons. The problem is not the question but the form in which it is asked. There is a presumption that *higher* means *better*. This is not correct. But, while *a higher degree* does not mean a better or more important degree, I can understand why some might ask this question.

I well remember visiting large Masonic gatherings in my years of Masonry. They were mostly national gatherings. A few brothers always walked around with medals filling nearly every inch of their jackets. Because of the manner in which they walked, held themselves, and their number of medals, these brothers clearly gave the impression that they were *very* important. The unspoken message was that if you had not attained every possible degree and belonged to every possible organization, then you were not as good as these *important* brothers. This message was received by all who saw these power brokers, and it was believed by far more than we might imagine. What a shame. This type of nonsense must be understood for what it is and dismissed. Masonry's goal is self-improvement, not determining who will sink the fastest in a lake because of all the metal being worn.

Freemasonry is not about titles, degrees or offices held. It is about improving yourself and being of service to our fellow human beings. We must never fall in the trap of being a *somebody* who everyone must look up to in awe.

But there are certain facts about degrees that we must face. Without any judgment of value, if you have a string of numbers, then 27 will be *higher* than 12. That is just the progression of the numbers. It is not a judgment. It does not mean that one number is better than or superior to another. It is simply counting.

Craft Masonry is today associated with the first three degrees, but this was not the case with the old Operative Freemasons. In a lodge of Operative Masons, some were learning their craft and perfecting the skills necessary for their advancement. These were the *apprentices*. When they completed their apprenticeship, they would present their work, known as their *masterpiece,* for evaluation. If their work proved acceptable, they would be worthy of joining the *fellows of the craft*. The master oversaw the lodge. Wardens may have been supervisors. So, there would seem to be a general correlation between the old Operative and Speculative lodges. But Speculative Freemasonry has added degrees and various rites to the system. Regardless of the additions, no *higher* degree should be viewed as *better*.

Let's look at the question *higher* or *better* from another perspective. Let's say that during a six-month period you have two people who have read the same book. During the same time, one of them read no other book, but the second person read four additional books. No matter how you look at it, the individual who read five books has been exposed to more literature than the one who read only one. This does not mean the one reading five books is better or more intelligent. It also does not mean the additional books were better than the first. It only means that one of them has read more books.

One who has received the Master Mason degree has, in the United States, fulfilled the craft degrees. He has advanced as far in craft Masonry as anyone can advance. Yes, both the Scottish Rite and York Rite offer additional degrees, but these are beyond the craft lodge. These additional degrees offer us more Light (information or experiences) in Masonry. There is no way to get around that fact. If one receives his Master Mason Degree and then joins his local Valley of the Scottish Rite, he will advance to the 32nd degree. At some point, he may also receive the 33rd degree. If so, he will have received all the degrees he can receive in the Scottish Rite. But, if he then decides to take the degrees of the York Rite, he will receive a whole new set of degrees and experiences.

More degrees do not mean a better or more important Mason. It means that this Mason has received more experiences or Light in Masonry. Additional degrees also do not guarantee any understanding of the symbolism in the degrees received. The only thing of which we can be certain is that one who takes additional degrees has been exposed to more degrees. If your eyes are closed, the additional Light means nothing. We must understand that there are (and have been) Masons of outstanding ability, service, and quality who never went beyond the Master Mason degree. There is no connection between how many degrees you have received and your value to or your understanding of Freemasonry. But it does mean that you have exposed yourself to more Light and experiences in Masonry. That, by itself, is of value, but it does not make you better or more important than someone else. The quality of a man is what he does with what he has. The goal of a Mason is never to stop growing.

In a gentle way, you can shake the world

~ Mahatma Gandhi

Being the Worshipful Master

Leadership is the capacity to translate vision into reality.
~ Warren Bennis

Thoughts often arise concerning the role and position of the Worshipful Master. How does a Worshipful Master maintain order in the lodge? How does he walk the line of maintaining authority but not stray into abuse? Experience is a very good instructor, but many times (too many for comfort), young Masons are pushed into this office with only a few years of membership under their belt. Good intentions and raw talent may not be enough if events happen to test them and their ability.

There are few things that can destroy a lodge faster than a Worshipful Master who has allowed power to go to his head or has allowed the position to control him. Many times, the problems come from a lack of understanding of the nature and responsibilities of such an office. Other times it can be personality quirks where one simply seeks and needs power. Let's say that there is a belief that your Worshipful Master is abusing his office. In that case, you should first seek the counsel of Past Masters or District Officers. You should try and understand if actual abuse is occurring or if it is misunderstandings. One-on-one talks are often constructive. If it is felt that the possibility of abuse is taking place, then it is a serious matter. You should contact the District Deputy Grand Master or other Grand Lodge officers as they may be needed to see what steps can be taken to correct the situation.

There are certain things, in jurisdictions with which I am familiar, which are not allowed to be done by a Worshipful Master. One thing a Worshipful Master is not allowed to do is reprimand a brother in open lodge without a trial. If, following a Masonic trial, a Mason is found guilty of an offense, reprimand in open lodge is one of the verdicts that can be given. So, if a Worshipful Master did reprimand a member in open lodge and no trial had taken place, then this would be an abuse of his office.

A Worshipful Master should use care in his words and actions in open lodge. If, for example, a member of the lodge is speaking out of turn or in other ways disruptive, a tap of the gavel by the Worshipful Master and a reminder to come to order should be enough to resolve the situation. If this action is not enough to resolve the situation, then it is proper to gavel the brother up and remind him to come to order. If all else fails, the Worshipful Master can tell him, "Brother, you are instructed to retire from the lodge." The Senior Deacon will normally escort the brother out. While this action is appropriate as a last resort, it would not be appropriate to follow this up with anything along the lines of "You should be ashamed of yourself." "You are not acting like a Mason." "You must learn how to conduct yourself in lodge" or any words which appear to be a reprimand.

Abuse of power can create problems across the board, and I have seen the destruction of a lodge due to the acts of an abusive Worshipful Master. If you witness such an event in your lodge, bring it up to someone. Let others in positions of authority know exactly what happened so that the matter might have a better chance of being resolved.

One of the obvious problems that can lead to abuse of power comes from the speed at which a Mason can become a Worshipful Master. Realistically, someone can join a lodge and, within just a year or two, can be elected Worshipful Master. They simply have not had the time to learn all that needs to be learned, not only with the ritual, but the practices and laws of the jurisdiction. They have not seen enough problems in lodges and how the problems were resolved. But not only is there a risk of their being abusive, but it can also go to the other end of the spectrum, and they may not know how to be firm enough in lodge.

Anyone who is in line for the office of Worshipful Master should try to attend as many lodges as are practical. They should expose themselves to as many lodge meetings as possible to maximize potential problems and witness the resolution of the problems. They should read as many books as they can lay their hands on dealing with lodge practices, lodge procedures, and, of course, they should be very familiar with their own Grand Lodge rules and regulations.

When sitting in the East, an odd feeling comes over you — especially when you are new to the office. Everyone in the lodge seems to be looking at you and watching every move you make. Every word you say feels under scrutiny. Nerves can come into play, and you may sometimes find it difficult to talk. Of course, you may find that the very best answers to questions or situations will come to you two or three days after the event has passed. It will only be then that you realize the best answer.

Regardless of nerves or insecurities, a wise Worshipful Master must realize that peace and harmony must always be maintained in a lodge. If a problem develops which can result in the loss of that peace and harmony, then the Master must take steps to preserve the dignity of the lodge.

Let's look at an event I witnessed some years ago. I was visiting a lodge, and the meeting was going smoothly. The Worshipful Master spoke on how the air conditioning system had been malfunctioning. He called upon a committee that had been created to explore the question of repairing or replacing air conditioning. It was an important discussion as either would cost a good deal of money. The chairman of the committee made his report and gave the recommendation of the committee. The Master then called for comments on the matter. Some spoke in favor of the recommendation, and some were against it. Finally, one brother requested to speak, and the Master gave him the floor. Instead of speaking on the air conditioning, he announced an event with another body taking place the following month and he had tickets available for anyone who might want to attend. The Master, quite correctly, informed him that he was out of order. He said that the matter being discussed was the committee's report, and if he wished to offer his tickets, he could do so after the vote of the lodge. From across the lodge, a brother boomed out, "No! I want to hear about this event. Go on brother, continue telling us about these tickets." The Master quietly sat back in his chair and the one with the tickets finished his announcement. I was dumbfounded.

After the lodge meeting, I learned that the one who yelled out his instructions was something of the lodge "kingpin." He was a Past Master who, for some reason, felt that regardless of who occupied the East, *he* was the actual authority in the lodge. Everyone occupying the East understood his *position* and yielded to him whenever he required it. The situation was a failure from beginning to end.

When the unruly brother boomed out his instructions, a responsible and experienced Worshipful Master should have dropped the gavel and instructed everyone that the non-related discussion was over as it was out of order. That would be the end of the matter. If a brother felt the need to continue to challenge the Master and would not allow the matter to drop, it would then be advisable, in his case, to place the lodge at refreshment and deal with the matter outside of a lodge at labor. A wise Master should do all in his power to keep disturbances out of a lodge at labor.

The Master controls the lodge, but he always seeks the balance between making it clear that *he* is the Worshipful Master and not being abusive. A successful Worshipful Master projects an aura of confidence backed up by his knowledge of the work and procedures. No Worshipful Master should be unfair, unyielding, or unwilling to listen to the counsel of others.

A successful Worshipful Master knows the value of "taking a beat." This means that when something happens, they do not immediately respond. They take a beat, process what has happened, and compose their thoughts. "What has just happened?" "What is going on?" "What is the best response?" If you take a beat when something happens, you have a better chance of avoiding a knee-jerk reaction and saying something that may have been better left unsaid.

In all cases, the Worshipful Master is responsible for the proper work of the lodge. Unruly members must be reduced to order. If no other solution is available, an unruly member should be removed from the lodge. In doing so, the Master should act firmly yet make it clear that his goal is to maintain order in the lodge and that his actions are in the lodge's best interest. It should never be personal. The Master should not be unfair to an unruly member *or* the lodge. Allowing anything at all to go on in the lodge is not in the lodge's best interest. Weak leadership can result in failure of the lodge just like if the Master were an abusive dictator.

Of course, any step or action taken which goes against the wishes of some can result in hard feelings. If bad feelings develop because one simply does not understand how Masons should act in lodge, or the proper role of the Worshipful Master, then the Master should take the extra step to try and talk with him. He should try to make it clear to the member that no attempt to single him out, hurt his feelings, or be unfair was being made. But the Master must realize that he is responsible for the lodge, and keeping order is necessary. When questions develop, the Master should seek the advice of knowledgeable and seasoned Past Masters or Grand Lodge officers.

Many books and resources are available for Worshipful Masters to learn ways to avoid problems and enjoy a successful year. Often overlooked aspects of demeanor, dress, and tone of voice will play a part if the membership respects you initially or if you have an uphill battle to fight. If you do not know the ritual, there may be a presumption that you also do not know the rules and laws. When you make a ruling, doubt of your abilities may result in challenges. This is just another reason why a Worshipful Master who is proficient in the ritual, who is professional in his dress and conduct, and giving all signals that he is in control will have a far easier time than someone who is not confident in what they are doing or, worse yet, does not care what they are doing.

If you don't seem to care, they won't care.

Success is not final, failure is not fatal:
it is the courage to continue that counts.

~ Winston S. Churchill

My Story of Discovering the Present Day Supreme Council of LouisianaError! Bookmark not defined.

The real voyage of discovery consists not in seeking new landscapes, but in having new eyes.

~ Marcel Proust

I joined Freemasonry in New Orleans in 1975. Like most all who join, my actual knowledge of Masonry at that time was very limited and superficial. I had several family members who were Masons, but I really knew only the very basics of the nature of Freemasonry and certainly not much in the area of Masonic history. Several years later, I joined the Valley of New Orleans. I knew even less about the Scottish Rite. I did, however, know one thing very clearly — I was impressed to no end with the Masonic philosophy and ritual, especially concerning the Scottish Rite.

While I was very impressed with the Scottish Rite, there was another aspect of which I became quickly aware. The Valley of New Orleans was, for lack of a better term, an emotional place. Laughter in the valley could be quick, deep, and genuine. But at the same time, there was a cloud of hurt and anger that always seemed present and could surface almost any time. I didn't understand why at the time, but the emotion in the valley was tangible.

My craft lodge had two members who were 33rds in the New Orleans Valley. In itself, that is not such an unusual accomplishment as many lodges can boast of members who hold the 33rd degree. What was, however, very unusual about these members was the title in the Scottish Rite that they both held. They were both Past Grand Masters of Kadosh of the Grand Consistory of Louisiana. That's a title you don't hear every day. You see, from 1811[1] until 1973 (just several years before I joined), the Valley of New Orleans was the Grand Consistory of Louisiana. The presiding officer of the Grand Consistory was the Grand Master of Kadosh. In 1973, Sovereign Grand Commander Henry Clausen downgraded the Grand Consistory of Louisiana (the last grand consistory under the Southern Jurisdiction) into a statutory consistory of the Valley of New Orleans.[2] This action of abolishing the Grand Consistory can explain much (but not all) of the bad feelings in the valley at the time of my joining. There was a general feeling that much was being, and had been, unfairly taken from New Orleans.

Whenever I talk on this subject, the question often arises, "What is a grand consistory?" To give you a little background, a grand consistory is a Scottish Rite body subordinate to a supreme council but superior to lodges of perfection or other Scottish Rite bodies. In the grand lodge system, you might think of a grand consistory as something along the lines of a provincial grand lodge. Its job was to provide local supervision to bodies under the jurisdiction of the supreme council but at a considerable distance from the council itself.[3] The collective voice and vote of a grand consistory carried the same authority as a Sovereign Grand Inspector General. The Valley of New Orleans, and that includes its time as the Grand Consistory of Louisiana, is the oldest continually active high-grade body of Ancient and Accepted Scottish Rite Masonry in North or South America.

Another body that I learned about soon after joining the Valley of New Orleans was a body identified to me as the "New Orleans Supreme Council." Wow, what a collection of stories I remember learning about this body! And, what an exercise in contradiction. After reading a few of the books and documents and listening to members, I had no idea in the world who or what to believe concerning this body. When I listened to the stories told by some of the then senior members of the valley, I learned of a near-mythical body akin to a Shangri-La or Camelot where everything was done correctly. Everyone was wise & kind, and all were content. But then, the stories continued, others became jealous of this utopian paradise. Outsiders wished the New Orleans Scottish Rite harm and sought all that they possessed. The New Orleans Scottish Rite Masons were tricked, lied to, and destroyed just so that everything good about them could be taken away.

Interestingly enough, there was another side to that coin and a *very* different story. When I read any of the old Scottish Rite history books, and that included the grand-daddy of all Louisiana Masonic history books, *Outline of the Rise and Progress of Freemasonry in Louisiana*, a completely different tale was told. In these accounts, it was the New Orleans Supreme Council who were the bad guys. It was not just a body of Masons who held a different view of Masonry, nor was it simply an irregular body. The New Orleans

Supreme Council was a collection of morally corrupt gangsters. They were portrayed as near monsters who would steal the Masonic souls of the naive and foolish, all so that they could practice their perverted Scottish Rite abomination.

I couldn't believe what I was reading and hearing. This was not just a little difference of opinion; the stories were complete spectrum opposites. The "other guys" were not just wrong but pure evil! I was absolutely fascinated. I also found it amazing that both sides offered their arguments with an outrageous lack of evidence and always with extreme emotion. The *only* thing that both sides agreed upon was that this supreme council died off in the late 1800s.

There was no question in my mind — I *had* to do my own research into this astonishing historical puzzle. I just needed a place to start.

My first goal was to collect and study as many of the old Masonic and Scottish Rite history books as I could find. Most were long out of print. I visited used bookstores as well as Masonic, public, and university libraries. When I could not buy a book, I would find one in a library or elsewhere and photocopy it. I spent months pouring over these books. The next step was to try and locate as many of the documents mentioned in the books as possible. I contacted the then Grand Secretary of the Grand Lodge of Louisiana, RW Brother Jack Crouch, and the then Sovereign Grand Inspector General in Louisiana, Ill Brother D. Walter Jessen, and asked both for letters of introduction. Both kindly gave me wonderful letters, which allowed me to contact grand lodges and supreme councils with questions and requests for aid in my search.

As my search for documents continued, I began to realize that it was necessary for me to travel to various locations and do "boots on the ground" research (the internet did not exist in those days). I visited both the Southern Jurisdiction and Northern Masonic Jurisdiction in my quest. Both supreme council visits brought me valuable documents from which I gained insight, but my trip to the Southern Jurisdiction brought much more.

I was in communication with Dr. John Boettcher, the then Editor of the *Scottish Rite Journal*, for some time. The communications normally concerned things I had written and were published in both the *Scottish Rite Journal* and its earlier incarnation, *The New Age*. I also worked on several research projects with the then Librarian of the House of the Temple, Mrs. Inge Baum. I contacted Dr. Boettcher and made plans for a visit. I explained that I was looking for any documents relating to early Scottish Rite Masonry in Louisiana and the troubled times of the "Scottish Rite war" before and after the Concordat of 1855.[4]

Upon arriving at the House of the Temple, I was greeted by Dr. Boettcher. He gave me a tour of the massive building. As we walked into the library, I was impressed with the extensive collection of books. But really, I expected nothing less. We were greeted by a slight, elderly lady smiling from ear to ear; it was Mrs. Baum. After a few friendly words, she led me to a long, beautiful table that took up a large portion of the room. The table had chairs on both sides and at the head and foot. I noticed a large stack of papers right to the side of the head of the table. This is where Mrs. Baum was leading me. She pointed at the papers and told me that this was the collection of Louisiana documents that I had requested. There was an odd smile and look in her eyes. She then asked me if I knew why she had placed the documents in that particular spot on the table. I told her that I had no idea. She then said with a large smile that this was where the last person who requested Louisiana documents always sat when he studied them. She then asked me if I knew who she was speaking about. I told her that I did not. With an even larger smile, she said, "Mr. Clausen." With a bit of surprise, I asked her if she meant Past Sovereign Grand Commander Henry Clausen. She said yes and that he came to the library several times a week, sat in that spot, and studied anything and everything that he could find concerning the Louisiana Scottish Rite and Louisiana Masonry. I was more than surprised and filed that information away for later consideration.

On the same trip, I planned on visiting the Grand Lodge of the District of Columbia. I had communicated a number of times with the then Grand Secretary, MWBro Stewart Miner, and became friendly with him. He was very interested in Masonic research and greatly assisted me in researching his grand lodge's archives. During my visit, MWBro Miner told me he wanted me to meet several young researchers with whom he had become acquainted over the last few years. He said one, in particular, had also shown great interest in researching the early history of the Scottish Rite. He was a Texas Mason by the name of Arturo de Hoyos. Over the next few years, Art and I would become good friends and make trips to the House of the Temple together in search of Scottish Rite documents. We also spent countless hours on the phone discussing the "lost history" of the Scottish Rite. Bro. de Hoyos shared my interest in the enigma of the New

Orleans Supreme Council. It was an amazing academic, Masonic detective mystery.

As I began to delve deeper into the books and documents concerning the troubled Scottish Rite times of the mid-1800s and the heartbreaking war that turned Brother against Brother, an extraordinarily depressing picture started emerging. The language in the books, from both sides, was akin to spitting acid. It didn't matter if it were James Foulhouze, Albert Pike, or whoever was writing; it was all so very harsh. I felt physically ill when I would stop and realize that these were *Masons* speaking to and about other Masons. I had never read anything that reached this level of near hatred. Every possible insult, attack, and nastiness was levied against "the other guys" simply because they existed. No one would give an inch. Looking from the outside, I could see that neither side was completely right or wrong. The only thing that both sides shared was that *neither* were acting very Masonic. The heart of the problem seemed to be ego. Neither side could admit that they could be in *any way* wrong or the other in *any way* right. They both sacrificed Masonry for pride. It was truly the saddest collection of documents I had ever read. All they had to do was put their hand out and welcome the other. The fact that they were both living in glass houses and both insistent on throwing rocks seemed to escape them. Honestly, there were no winners in that war.

Some months later (early 1994), on a visit to the Grand Lodge of Louisiana, I was asked by the Grand Secretary if I could take over communicating with someone who I was told was a "French Brother living in Germany." I was told that the brother had shown great interest in the early history of Louisiana Masonry but was asking questions that no one in the Grand Lodge office could answer. I was shown the last letter the brother wrote. I recognized the name immediately. It was WBrother Alain Bernheim.

Over the next months and years, Bro. Bernheim and I became good friends. We would write to each other regularly (starting with postal mail and then e-mail), sharing information on Masonic research with special attention to the early history of Louisiana Freemasonry and its Scottish Rite. In one mail to Bro Bernheim, I wrote about how I felt it was such a shame that a body that seemed to be so very regular and Masonic in nature as the New Orleans Supreme Council could cease to exist. I lamented the loss of this historic and significant body. He wrote me back a very short e-mail. He said that he only had two questions for me. The first was why did I continually call that body the "New Orleans Supreme Council" when their correct name is "The Supreme Council of Louisiana?" The second question was, why did I continually say that they no longer existed?

I was stunned. As to the first question, I called them that because that was how I had always heard them called in New Orleans. I knew their official name but used the common term that I had repeatedly heard used. As to the second astonishing question, I told Bro. Bernheim, I assumed they no longer existed because I have never heard or read a single word to the contrary. I had never seen a scrap of evidence to suggest that they still existed. He wrote back, saying that I was in New Orleans, and he was halfway around the world. He said that if I am so sure of their non-existence, then the accounts he learned of must be incorrect.

I remember sitting in the chair at my desk, thinking about my exchange with Bro. Bernheim. How ridiculous. I had been a Mason by that time for some 20 years in New Orleans. Not once did I *ever* hear anything of the supreme council still existing. But what a resounding kick in the pants it would be if they did exist. As I was sitting there, I looked over at the telephone book on my desk. I stared at it for a time and then laughed to myself. It simply could not be possible that they were listed in the phone book. That was too easy. I could no longer help myself, I had to look. I picked up the phone book and flipped through the pages.

I cannot tell you exactly how I felt next. I imagine the best way to describe it was the old image of someone falling out of their chair in shock. There in the phone book, as big as life was listed, *"The Supreme Council of Louisiana."* What in the world was going on? Was I in an episode of *The Twilight Zone*? I just sat there for a little while, totally bewildered. Then I did the only thing I could think of doing. I picked up the phone and called the number listed. They answered the phone, *"Supreme Council of Louisiana."* I had no idea what to say. Finally, I said that I had a question to ask. I asked if they were the same supreme council that was created in 1839. The voice on the phone came back with, "Yes, we are." I thanked him and hung up. What in the world was going on? I had by then spent many years digging into the early history of a body that I *thought* had ceased to exist in the late 1800s. Am I now to believe that they still exist? How stupid could I be? But, in my defense, not *once* did I *ever* see, hear, or read *anything* to suggest that they still existed. And, really, what proof did I have that they did still exist? Anyone can list a phone under whatever name they like. That's no proof at all. So, I grabbed my keys, went out to the car, and drove to the address given in the phone book.

I recognized the building as I drove up. I had passed by it many times over the years, noticed the signs, but never paid much attention to it. I had always assumed that it was some fly-by-night Masonic self-creation. I parked the car and went inside. There were several African-American men inside, and one introduced himself as the Secretary-General. He then introduced me to the Sovereign Grand Commander, Philip Washington, Sr. I introduced myself and told them that I had been researching the early history of the Scottish Rite and Freemasonry in Louisiana. I felt a bit uncomfortable as I had no idea if this could possibly be the real deal or if they had simply found some old documents or records and created a body with an old name. In other words, I didn't know if they were frauds or not.

We talked just a little, and most of it was superficial. I then asked if they had a list of their Sovereign Grand Commanders from the time of their creation. The secretary said that he thought he had something like that around. He looked through his desk and pulled out a piece of paper. He made a photocopy of it and gave me a copy. I thanked them all and left.

When I got home, I looked at the paper I was given (See: Appendix D & E). It started with a list of names that I knew well. But, after Eugene Chassaignac, began a long list of names that I had never seen before. At that time, I noticed something that gave me reason to believe that the body I had just visited was, indeed, a self-created, fraudulent body. Following Eugene Chassaignac were 19 names listed as

Sovereign Grand Commanders. 17 of the names were printed with the last two (Joseph Williams, 1987 and Philip Washington, Sr., 1993) handwritten onto the list. The last printed name was George Longe, showing that he was elected Sovereign Grand Commander in 1938. That's almost 50 years between the election of George Longe and Joseph Williams. Prior to George Longe, most Sovereign Grand Commanders served only a few years. I had no idea how long George Longe served, but it seemed likely that *maybe* he served until sometime around WWII, and then the council died off to be recreated in 1987 by Joseph Williams.

What interested me most, at the time, were the 17 printed names (some serving more than once) that followed Eugene Chassaignac. If these names were proven to actually be Sovereign Grand Commanders of the Supreme Council of Louisiana, then it would mean that the council existed far longer than had previously been believed. I wanted to find a way to check out these names and any possible association with the council. I went to the public library.

The New Orleans Public Library has provided me with a great deal of help in the past. Their main library had a microfilm section with most all the old newspapers published in New Orleans in the 1800s. My idea was to look up the death notices in the old papers for each of the names listed and to see if I could find anything of interest. To my amazement, for each and every name I searched, I found a death notice published in the newspaper by the Supreme Council of Louisiana. The notices were announcing the death of their Sovereign Grand Commander. Every single name was accounted for, and each carried a death notice from the council. It seemed that the Supreme Council of Louisiana had existed far longer than had been known. I realized that this was a major discovery. How they could have existed all this time with no record of their existence was a question I put aside for a later time. I then came to the name of George Longe. As I began the search for his death notice, I realized that, with this information, I would likely find the actual date of the death of the Supreme Council of Louisiana.

Earlier, I mentioned a discovery that was so surprising to me that I almost fell out of my chair. Well, that was when I was in the privacy of my home, sitting at my desk. For the same thing to happen to me in a public library was considerably more embarrassing. I found the death notice of George Longe. Like the others, it carried a notice from the Supreme Council of Louisiana. But George Longe didn't die until late 1985. My mind was whirling. If the council died in the 30s, 40s, or 50s, how could it announce his death in 1985?[5] Does this mean that George Longe served as Sovereign Grand Commander for almost 50 years? Does this mean that the body I visited is *actually* the very same supreme council that I learned about when I joined Masonry?

There were simply too many questions for me to deal with at that time. I needed a bit of time to process everything and think about the information in a logical and structured manner. I decided to take some time off and let things sink in and only then formulate my next steps. But, sometimes, things go differently than we plan.

In boxing, there is something known as a one-two punch. The first part of that punch came at the library with the discovery concerning George Longe. The second part of the punch came the very next day. I went early to the

University of New Orleans to pick up a French-to-English translation of an old Masonic document that I had found some time back. I was able to make my way through many of the old French writings, but when I suspected something was important, I would call on a friend of mine who was a French Professor at the university. I spoke to him about some of the discoveries. He was not a Mason but was very interested in Masonic history. He told me that I really should go to the history department and speak with one of the instructors there. She had recently received her PhD, and a good part of her dissertation was on, of all things, early Louisiana Freemasonry, especially Scottish Rite Freemasonry in New Orleans. I walked over to the history department and met Dr. Caryn Cossé Bell.[6] We talked for a while, and I gave her a few names of key figures in my research. She knew them all. I then asked her if she knew of George Longe. She said she knew of him well and asked if I visited "his collection" at Tulane University. I had not and didn't even know that it existed. Dr. Bell gave me directions to the building to find the collection, and I was off like a shot.

When I arrived at Tulane, I went to find the collection.[7] If I tried to explain how I felt when I saw what was in that collection, I imagine the best way to describe it is to think of that little boy upon first arriving in Willy Wonka's candy factory. I was overwhelmed. It was not just a large collection of Scottish Rite documents; it was a large collection of *very important* Scottish Rite documents. To give just one example, I found what is today known as *The Bonseigneur Rituals* within that collection.[8] It is a collection of 18th-century New Orleans Ecossais Masonic Rituals. Upon finding them, I sent a copy of these rituals to Alain Bernheim for dating. I also sent a copy to Gerald Prinsen of the Latomia Foundation in the

Netherlands for publication. The rituals are a hand-written copy of a much older collection of rituals. The copy is dated as being made about 1785 to the early 1790s, and some of the rituals look to date prior to 1750. Even with this aside, it is very possibly the lost rituals of the Grand Lodge of Louisiana, being worked by the Grand Lodge and the five French-speaking lodges that created it. This significant find was made in *their* collection. To this day, I have yet to completely explore all the collection.

The first thing I did upon entering the collection was to pull out that list of Sovereign Grand Commanders and search for each of them. I was able to find letters, documents, diplomas, and other official records for each of them signing as the Sovereign Grand Commander of the Supreme Council of Louisiana. Yep, George Longe served as Sovereign Grand Commander for almost 50 years! There was now no doubt, the body known today as the Supreme Council of Louisiana is the very same body from the 1800s. But, apart from a footnote, what does it mean? Then, years later, came 2011.

It was the 200th anniversary of the creation of the Grand Consistory of Louisiana — the one valley of high-grade Ancient and Accepted Scottish Rite Freemasonry that continued to exist when all others in the United States slumbered. A foresighted Scottish Rite Honorary Sovereign Grand Inspector General and Past Grand Master of the Grand Lodge of Louisiana, Clayton J. Borne, III, felt that a celebration was in order and appointed me to the planning committee. He obtained permission and organized a Scottish Rite symposium where the Scottish Rite could be celebrated and studied using public lectures on the Scottish Rite. I had spoken many times about the Supreme Council of Louisiana.

We thought that an invitation for them to attend such a celebration was in order.

On June 1st to 4th, 2011, for the first time in history, representatives of the Supreme Council, Southern Jurisdiction, USA; the Supreme Council of Louisiana and the Grand Lodge of Louisiana joined together with the representatives of other supreme councils and Grand Lodges to meet at the Royal Sonesta Hotel on Royal Street in New Orleans ... and peace and harmony prevailed. The symposium location was just steps away from where Albert Mackey met with James Foulhouze in Mackey's failed attempt to have Foulhouze join the Southern Jurisdiction.[9] There was no ritual, no "secrets" exchanged, no compromising situations. It was a public gathering that was, in this writer's experience, the most truly Masonic gathering I have ever attended. It was beautiful.

Through knowledge, we now have an opportunity. We will own the choices we make. But what will we do? Continue a pointless "war," continue a policy of "hidden in plain sight," or respect others who do the true work of the Scottish Rite? Do we battle against ourselves or against ignorance?

The beauty of the future is that it is an open book upon which we can write whatever path we choose. We now know far more about this aspect of our Scottish Rite history than we knew not too many years ago. And, with that knowledge, we can do whatever we like. The future of the Scottish Rite is up to us. I truly hope that we can put all the pain, misinformation, ego, and nonsense aside and once again become what the creators of Freemasonry knew *as* Freemasonry. I have deep faith in the Scottish Rite.

Notes:

1. The earliest known appearance of the Grand Consistory of Louisiana was in New Orleans in 1811. There are, unfortunately, no known surviving minutes or documents from this body. Most of the information that has been collected concerning the 1811 Grand Consistory is recorded in a few secondary sources. James Scot gives us, in his 1873 *Outline of the Rise and Progress of Freemasonry in Louisiana*, a piece of information concerning this body by reproducing a communication dated 20 April 1811 from the Sov. Grand Consistory of Princes of the Royal Secret of Louisiana to Etoile Polaire Lodge. The communication seeks to establish relations between the Grand Consistory and Etoile Polaire Lodge. It is issued under the name of "Des Bois, Grand Secretary." (See: James Scot, *Outline of the Rise and Progress of Freemasonry in Louisiana* 1873 [New Orleans, LA: Cornerstone Book Publishers, reprint 2008.] pp. 21-22). Also, in his 1882 "Official Bulletin V," Albert Pike tells us that on March 28, 1811, the Grand Consistory of Louisiana was granted a charter by Louis Jean Lusson and Jean Baptiste Modeste Lefebvre, both SGIGs of the Supreme Council of Kingston, Jamaica. Pike also tells us that the Grand Consistory held its first meeting on Sunday, April 7, 1811, at 5 p.m. in the hall of Perfect Union Lodge. The meeting was attended by many of the "founding fathers" of Louisiana Freemasonry, who were Members of this Grand Consistory. (See: Albert Pike, *Official Bulletin of the Supreme Council of the 33rd Degree for the Southern Jurisdiction of the United States*. Washington, D.C. 1882). For many years 1813 was given as the creation date (incorrectly) for the Grand Consistory of Louisiana. This was the year the Grand Consistory passed under the jurisdiction of the Cerneau Sovereign Grand Consistory (supreme council) in New York. The Cerneau system used different names for some of their bodies. This is why from 1813 to the early 1830s, the surviving Minutes of the Grand Consistory of Louisiana show that it was known as the Grand COUNCIL of Louisiana. It was still a body of the 32nd degree but used a different name. So strong was the attachment to Cerneau by the Louisiana Masons that they seemed to have "forgotten" the time of their existence before Cerneau. (*Minutes Book of the Grand Consistory of Louisiana* [1822-1846]). Located in the *New Orleans Scottish Rite Bodies*. New Orleans, Louisiana.) See also: Michael R. Poll, "The Early Years of the Grand Consistory of Louisiana (1811-1815)." *Heredom Vol. 8*, (Washington, D.C., The Scottish Rite Research Society, 1999-2000) pp. 39-53., Arturo de Hoyos, "The Early Years of the Grand Consistory of Louisiana (1811-1815) - A Rejoinder" & Michael R. Poll, "A

Few 'Rejoinder' Comments." Both: *Heredom Vol. 9*, (Washington, D.C., The Scottish Rite Research Society, 2001) pp. 69-110.

2. "For multiple reasons, I directed that the Grand Consistory of Louisiana be converted into a statutory consistory of the Valley of New Orleans. I outlined the required procedure and our Grand Secretary General processed the necessary papers. Grand Consistories were inaugurated when communications over long distances were difficult. Later they were found to be impediment to effective administration so became outmoded. All except Louisiana had been converted into statutory consistories. There is no longer any sanction under our Statues for a Grand Consistory." - Henry C. Clausen, 33°, Sovereign Grand Commander. See: *Transactions of the Supreme Council, 33° for the Southern Jurisdiction, USA* (Washington, D.C., Supreme Council, 33° Southern Jurisdiction, USA, 1973) p. 46.

3. See: Albert Mackey, *An Encyclopedia of Freemasonry* (New York , NY, The Masonic History Company, 1925), p. 305.

4. See: Ray Baker Harris, James D. Carter, *History of the Supreme Council, 33° Southern Jurisdiction, USA (1801-1861)* (Washington, D.C., Supreme Council, 33° Southern Jurisdiction, USA, 1964) This Scottish Rite "war" centered itself on the reawakened "Charleston Supreme Council" (Supreme Council, Southern Jurisdiction, USA) and the "New Orleans Supreme Council" (Supreme Council of Louisiana). The two councils argued over regularity, with half of the Supreme Council of Louisiana signing a concordat in 1855 to pass under the jurisdiction of the Charleston Council and half refusing to participate. In 1856, the half of the Supreme Council of Louisiana, which refused to sign the concordat, announced that the signing of the Charleston concordat was illegal and that the Supreme Council of Louisiana continued to exist. In 1857, the powerful Past Sovereign Grand Commander, attorney, and judge, James Foulhouze, returned as Sovereign Grand Commander of the New Orleans Council. The Charleston Council answered with the young attorney, Albert Pike, being elected Sovereign Grand Commander in 1859 (the first *election* of a Grand Commander in the Charleston Council's history). The two went toe to toe in an epic battle equaling the Charleston/Cerneau battle some years earlier. See also: James Foulhouze, *Historical Inquiry into the Origins of the Ancient and Accepted Scottish Rite*, 1858, (New Orleans, LA: Cornerstone Book Publishers, reprint 2012).

5. It did not escape me that George Longe's death was in 1985, but the next Sovereign Grand Commander was not elected until 1987. I learned later that Longe was suffering from dementia for a number of years prior to his death. During this time, the Lt. Grand Commander assumed the day to

day duties of the Grand Commander and continued them until the 1987 election. It seems that the council was in something of a shock. Longe had served in office for so long and had been such a massive and successful figure in the council that there was uncertainty about how to carry on after his death. The only other time which seemed to have brought such sock to a supreme council was in the Southern Jurisdiction following the death of Albert Pike.

6. Dr. Bell's doctoral dissertation was first published (hardback) by the Louisiana State University Press in 1996. In 2004, it was released in paperback as *Revolution, Romanticism, and the Afro-Creole Protest Tradition in Louisiana, 1718-1868 (*Baton Rouge, LA Louisiana State University Press, 2004).

7. The George Longe Collection is located in *The Amistad Research Center* at Tulane University in New Orleans, LA. Online, the collection can be found at: http://www.amistadresearchcenter.org.

8. *The Bonseigneur Rituals*, (The Netherlands, The Latomia Foundation, 1996. Republished in the USA by Cornerstone Book Publishers, New Orleans, LA, 2008).

9. Michael R. Poll, "James Foulhouze: Sovereign Grand Commander of the Supreme Council of Louisiana" *Heredom Vol. 6*, (Washington, D.C., The Scottish Rite Research Society, 1997) pp. 64-69.

The "It" Factor (Just Do it)

I am not afraid of an army of lions led by a sheep;
I am afraid of an army of sheep led by a lion.
~ Alexander the Great

I remember a trip to my dad's office when I started high school (about a hundred years ago). He showed me a strange-looking new *thing* that he had on his desk. He called it a *Photostat machine*. It was intended to do away with the need for those nasty thin sheets of blue or black carbon paper which were placed in typewriters. A sheet of carbon paper would be sandwiched between two sheets of white typing paper, and you would type. The carbon paper would transfer whatever you typed on the top sheet to the bottom sheet. This would be done so that you could keep an ugly bluish or blackish copy of whatever you typed. But with this new machine, all you needed to do was type your letter, put it in the slot, and it would give you back an ugly brownish copy of your original. I thought it was the coolest thing ever. I immediately saw great possibilities. I gathered a few friends, and we started a newspaper. Sure, it looked horrible, but I had toured the offices of the large daily newspaper on a school field trip. I saw the equipment they had. How could I afford that kind of professional production? But, with this new machine, publishing a small newspaper became possible.

Yes, without question, I published an ugly-looking newspaper. I well remember the initial harsh criticism it received from some of the students and teachers. But that ugly little newspaper started to grow in popularity. This was because people began seeing past the delivery method to the actual message being conveyed in the paper. The message was sound and struck a chord with the readers. In my senior year, I left that little underground newspaper to become (over the objection of a few teachers) editor of the official high school newspaper, a position I would again hold for my college newspaper. These accomplishments would have been far more difficult to achieve had I not honed my skills with that little ugly Photostat newspaper. The whole experience taught me that *the message* is all important.

In my 40 years as a Mason, I have held many offices, received many awards, and been part of many organizations. But the service of which I am most proud is my part in creating The Masonic Society. In the summer of 2007, five Masons from different parts of the U.S. proposed a new Masonic research society. Silly, right? Pointless and a waste of time, right? Most Grand Lodges have either a research lodge or a research committee. There are also a number of well-respected Masonic research societies in the U.S. and abroad. I have no idea what made us think we could add anything to what was already in place. But we did think just that. We wrote to each other in joint e-mails and held a couple of phone conferences. We produced a plan and, in six months, opened the doors to The Masonic Society.

Oh, you can believe me, when we first opened the doors to our new little society, we had some *harsh* criticism from some in the establishment. Who did we think we were? How dare we do something like this with no permission from anyone? But you know what? It was just like my very early days with that ugly little newspaper. We struck a chord with far more of the U.S. Masons than we could have imagined. The Masonic Society had the "it" factor and took off like a rocket. Soon, many of our most harsh critics joined us and praised our work.

The point in recalling this story is to point out that it was not enough for five Masons to talk about a good idea, it took our acting on it for it to work. Failing to "just do it" is where so many of the brilliant ideas fail. Some of the most wonderful ideas I have ever heard went no further than words spoken. "I don't have the time," "I don't have enough support," "This or that leader won't support me" ... baloney. Just do it. If you know in your heart that it is Masonic, if you believe it is of value, then just do it. If it fails, then you pick yourself up and start over. You never, ever quit.

Mind you, I'm not at all suggesting that you violate any Masonic law or do something that you have been told not to do by your leadership. I'm saying that there are many things that can be done that only require your picking yourself up, stop talking about it, and do it. Don't look for the other guy to do something — *you* do it.

One more point; not every idea is a good idea. A campaign to ensure that all lodges have Masonic printed toilet paper might get far more laughs than support. Success is born out of failure. You need to recognize when something is just not going to make it and move on to another plan or idea. Never allow the few to turn you away from your idea, but also never allow your own ego to cause you to relentlessly push something that simply has no merit or value. You must always be brutally objective with yourself. My grandfather used to tell me, "It's never good to lie to others, but it's far worse to lie to yourself."

Masonry is a progressive moral science. You can't advance if you talk, but don't act on what you talk about. If you try it and it fails, move on to the next project. If you try it and it succeeds, move on to the next project. Never sit around and wallow in either your failures or successes. You need to just keep doing it ... again and again.

What would life be if we had no courage to attempt anything?

~ Vincent van Gogh

Masonic Communications

The single biggest problem in communication
is the illusion that it has taken place.
~ George Bernard Shaw

When I say something, the last thing I want is to be misunderstood. My goal is to always have the idea, thought, or desire in my head given to the other clearly and correctly. If I would like someone to walk three houses down from where I live to a certain address and ask Mr. Jones if I can borrow a hammer, it would not serve me very well if I pointed vaguely and said: "Go down there and bring me something from that guy." Where, what, who? If I want a particular thing (and not just anything), I need to be clear in communicating.

On the other hand, if I wish to teach using symbolism, then I will speak or write in a manner that will require the reader or listener to apply some thought to what I have offered. What is presented through symbolism may have more than one meaning and may not be evident by design. How I communicate depends on my desired goal. Language is a tool that should be employed with some thought as to the desired effect in each particular instance.

So, what do we mean when we speak of "Masonic Communications"? It is a fundamental question because, as Freemasons, we can't go having "Masonic Communications" with just anyone. We have obligations that must be kept. We must understand what can be communicated to others and what is not allowed.

Of "communication," Albert Mackey tells us:

> "The meeting of a Lodge is so called. There is a peculiar significance in this term. To communicate, which, in the Old English form, was to common, originally meant to share in common with others. The great sacrament of the Christian Church, which denotes a participation in the mysteries of the religion and a fellowship in the church, is called a communion, which is fundamentally the same as a communication, for be who partakes of the communion is said to communicate. Hence the meetings of Masonic Lodges are called communications, to signify that it is not simply the ordinary meeting of a society for the transaction of business, but that such meeting is the fellowship of men engaged in a common pursuit, and governed by a common principle, and that there is therein a communication or participation of those feelings and sentiments that constitute a true brotherhood."[1]

Our Work teaches us that we are not to hold "Masonic Communications" with non-Masons, or with unrecognized, irregular, or clandestine Masons. But what exactly does that mean to us today? It is clear through our law that someone who is a member of a lodge *not* in Fraternal Relations with our

Grand Lodge cannot attend our meetings,[2] but what are we allowed to say (communicate) to non-Masons, and what is to be kept secret?

The Handbook of Masonic Law (Louisiana) tells us the following about the nature of a "secret":

"Secrecy applies to the modes of recognition, certain symbols, the ballot, obligations, signs, passwords, and the forms of initiation."[3]

There we have it. We are not to reveal any of the above to anyone unless we are certain they are entitled to receive it. But who is entitled to receive it? We know that someone is entitled to receive "the secrets" if we have sat in Lodge with them or if they have successfully passed a trial as taught to us in our ritual. Most jurisdictions will have similar rules, but to be safe, check with your Grand Lodge.

So, exactly who are those who might be considered *unrecognized, irregular, or clandestine*? These are often words that are used in Masonry interchangeably — even officially by Grand Lodges. Are they interchangeable? What exactly do they mean? While these words can mean the same thing, they each have their own specific meaning and can sometimes mean very different things. We can run into confusion if we do not know when they can or can't be used interchangeably.

Fraternal Relations (recognition) is when two jurisdictions officially declare their satisfaction that each is regular. It is a treaty of friendship and acknowledgment that each is a legitimate Masonic body. It is a state that either exists, or it does not. It is simple to determine. The Grand

Lodge has a list of Masonic bodies which it "recognizes" and members who are allowed to visit our lodges, and with whom we may hold Masonic Communications — once we know them to be such. If a lodge is not on that list, they cannot visit tiled lodges under the jurisdiction of the Grand Lodge of Louisiana. But can we visit lodges with unrecognized Masons? Is there any situation where we can legally hold *Masonic Communications* with members of unrecognized lodges? The simple answer to the above questions is a surprising "yes" (at least in Louisiana, check your laws). It is sometimes called the "When in Rome Rule."

From the *Louisiana Handbook on Masonic Law*:

"Louisiana Masons, when traveling to other Grand Jurisdictions which are recognized as "Regular" by the Grand Lodge of the State of Louisiana, F.&A.M. and with which this Grand Lodge has established fraternal relations may, with the consent of the host Lodge or Grand Lodge, visit a tiled communication in any Lodge recognized as Regular by the Grand Lodge of Louisiana, F.&A.M. within that jurisdiction and, during the course thereof, exercise Masonic visitation with the Brethren who are recognized as Regular by that Grand Jurisdiction."[4]

This law was put in place due to the fact that of the "mainstream" Grand Lodges in the United States, the vast majority of them have entered into Fraternal Relations with the Prince Hall Affiliate Grand Lodge in their state. They consider Prince Hall Affiliate Masons perfectly regular. Louisiana is one of the states that has not entered into Fraternal Relations with the Prince Hall Grand Lodge in our state. As such, if the "When in Rome Rule" did not exist in our Grand Lodge law, visiting any of the lodges in those other Grand Lodges that recognize Prince Hall in their state could be a problem. We could be sitting in a lodge and holding Masonic Communications with Masons not recognized by our Grand Lodge. That would be grounds for Masonic charges of violating our obligations. How could our Grand Master or other Grand Lodge Officers visit other jurisdictions? So, does this mean that we do or do not view Prince Hall as regular?

Regularity is a subjective state. It is not as clear to determine as we might think and certainly not as easy to determine as recognition. Grand Lodges, after examination, determine if a body is, or is not, *regular* — and views on regularity can change.

In an attempt to make the whole situation a bit easier to understand, Grand Lodges, years ago, seemed to become fond of linking regularity with recognition. If a body was recognized, then it was viewed as regular. It was said to be irregular or clandestine if it was not recognized. Most of the time, this worked fine. But every now and then, we are bitten if we never allow for the exception. The "When in Rome Rule" is an example of how we can't always clearly look to recognition to determine regularity. Logic dictates that if the Grand Lodge of Louisiana considers Prince Hall Affiliate Masonry to be irregular, then our law presents a situation where we are allowed to hold Masonic Communications with those we consider to be irregular. Is that what we are saying? That would seem to be a violation of our Obligations.

Louisiana has an official written record of viewing at least one Grand Lodge regular with whom Fraternal Relations had not yet been established. If we look at the Grand Lodge of Louisiana Proceedings from 1955, we can find that Louisiana considered the National Grand Lodge in France to be regular. Yet, Fraternal Relations were not then offered or existing.[5] Yep, they were deemed *regular*, but they were not *recognized*. Lack of recognition *does not* always officially mean irregular.

To be irregular means that there is something wrong with the body. It could be a problem with the work, the linage (how they were created), or any other matter that would present a problem to anyone seeking to determine whether they are a valid Masonic body. It could be a minor, fixable problem or a problem of such severity that the body would be deemed hopeless and unable to be saved.

And what of the word "clandestine"? Yes, it is often used with or in place of "irregular." But it has a much more specific meaning. When the Soviet Union broke apart, an interesting thing happened. All of a sudden, hands started popping up. The hands belonged to Masonic lodges that had existed in the Soviet Union but were underground and hidden away. Freemasonry was outlawed, and had these lodges been discovered, the members would have been in considerable trouble. But they kept Freemasonry alive by working in secret. These are actual *clandestine* lodges — hidden lodges. Yes, they were irregular in the most technical sense as they operated under no Grand Lodge authority. But as soon as they were discovered, the European Grand Lodges lined up to take them in. They realized that the "problem" was an easy fix, and these Masons were worthy of great respect, not condemnation.

At the writing of this paper, Fraternal Relations between the Most Worshipful Grand Lodge of the State of Louisiana, F&AM, and the Most Worshipful Prince Hall Grand Lodge of Louisiana, F&AM does not exist. The law of the Grand Lodge of Louisiana is clear that members of lodges under any Grand Lodge with whom Fraternal Relations do not exist cannot sit in one of our tiled lodges. Yet, the law is also clear that situations can arise where it is permitted for members of lodges under the Grand Lodge of Louisiana to sit in tiled lodges with Masons under the jurisdiction of a Prince Hall Grand Lodge. When we sit in a tiled lodge, "Masonic Communications" (however we define it) is taking place. At the opening of this paper, I pointed out the problems that can arise when we are not clear in our desires. It would seem that a contradiction exists in our laws and obligations. On the one hand, we are clearly told that we *cannot* hold Masonic Communications with an unrecognized Mason. Yet, in another aspect of our law, we are told that we *are* allowed to hold Masonic Communications with unrecognized Masons under certain situations. Neither directive references the other nor explains the apparent contradiction.

Freemasonry in the United States is in a time of remarkable evolution. Electronic communications, in general, have dramatically changed with the advent of cell phones, the internet, and a host of new electronic gadgets. With the recognition of Prince Hall Masonry by most of the Grand Lodges in the United States, our understanding of Masonic Communications has, by practicality, undergone a reevaluation and resulted in an evolution of the practice. It is not a perfect solution and is open to numerous charges of contradictory and illogical practices, but it is a work in progress. It is a step.

Should the Grand Lodge of Louisiana and the Prince Hall Grand Lodge of Louisiana clear up this apparent contradiction and officially enter into Fraternal Relations? This writer has his personal opinion, but it is a question for the two Grand Lodges. What is it that they both desire?

Fraternal Recognition is a two-way street. *Both* sides must desire it and work to its end. So, what do we want? It is a question we must all answer sooner or later.

*The most important thing in communication is
hearing what isn't being said.
The art of reading between the lines
is a life long quest of the wise.*

~ Shannon L. Alder

NOTES:

1. Albert G. Mackey, *An Encyclopedia of Freemasonry and its Kindred Sciences Vol. I* (New York: The Masonic History Company, 1925) 170.

2. "One who is a member of a Lodge under the jurisdiction of a Grand Lodge not in fraternal relations with the Grand Lodge of Louisiana, shall not be permitted to visit any of the Lodge of Louisiana." *The Handbook of Masonic Law* (Alexandria, LA: The Grand Lodge of the State of Louisiana, F&AM 2012) 110.
3. Ibid., iv b
4. Ibid 110.
5. "We do not question the regularity of the French National Grand Lodge — their recognition by 41 of the Grand Lodges of the United States attests to that. We are not ready, however, to suggest that the Grand Lodge of Louisiana sever the cordial relationship of long standing with the Grand Lodge of France." *Proceedings of The Grand Lodge of the State of Louisiana Free and Accepted Masons* (New Orleans: Searcy & Pfaff, LTD., Printers, 1955) 180.

The Lodge of Perfection

(Consequences of the Quest for Perfection)

There is nothing noble in being superior to your fellow man;
true nobility is being superior to your former self.

~ Ernest Hemingway

The Scottish Rite degrees of the Lodge of Perfection span the fourth to fourteenth degrees. If we boil these degrees down, they are the continuation and completion of the Scottish Rite craft ritual and the discovery of the lost word. The degrees take us through a moral pathway of lessons where we are taught that we are ultimately responsible for ourselves and our own actions. We learn that we must act in certain ways if we are to expect positive results. This paper is not, however, intended to focus on the actual degrees of the Lodge of Perfection or a commentary on its philosophy which can be read in many of the books on this subject. I wanted to take a bit of a different direction with this paper and focus on an aspect that is often ignored but is an integral part of the philosophy — the consequences of the quest for perfection.

We are taught that Freemasonry is a moral organization that takes good men and makes them better. We must choose to join and then advance by degrees. The suggestion here is that step by step, we grow and become *better* (however that is defined). This is an essential aspect of all moral philosophies because while change is inevitable, positive change, or growth, is our choice. We don't have to do anything that we choose *not* to do. If desired, we must choose to walk the Masonic path. If Masons, or in this case, Scottish Rite Masons, are given the proper tools, they can use them to make the conscious decision to improve themselves when they do change.

In this case, we must remember that we are using the specific word *perfection*. What do we mean by that word? Very few humans will claim to be perfect. If they do, they are discounted as delusional. The *quest for perfection* can sometimes be misunderstood. If we think that we are striving for a final goal of perfection, then we can expect to live a very frustrating life. We will never reach such a goal. No human can expect to make perfection out of his life. The most we can hope for is to make positive changes until our last day on Earth.

Throughout history, many societies have pondered the idea of the quest for perfection. There is an old symbolic legend from the Orient which might be considered. The story is of a Buddhist monk by the name of Kobo Daishi. We learn that Kobo was an artist of great renown. His talent and the beauty of his work were known throughout the land. One day, village leaders asked Kobo to create a dragon to be placed on the arch of a newly built temple. Kobo accepted the task. As the dragon was being carved, villagers would come to watch the master at work, marveling at the beauty of the large piece of stone. As the work progressed, crowds began to gather to witness the transformation of the raw stone at the hands of Kobo. As the dragon was near completion, the whole village was there watching the incredible work being done. The dragon was magnificent. No one had ever seen a more beautiful or life-like statue. When Kobo hit the very last strike on the statue, everyone knew that they were looking at perfection. It was then that something completely unexpected and terrifying happened. The dragon began to move. It was coming to life. The expressions of delight on the faces of the crowd were replaced by shock and fear. As the dragon began to move its head and wings, the villagers began to run in terror. The story tells us that when the Heavens saw the dragon and realized it was perfect, the dragon was given life. Kobo, realizing what was happening, rushed down to the base of the statue where a bucket of paint had been placed and flung it up on the dragon. As soon as the paint hit the dragon, it froze and returned to stone. It was no longer perfect. And there, the dragon remained as a *stone statue* on the temple's arch for some five hundred years.

Inside this story, there is a lesson offered to us. We are taught that there are consequences for perfection or, at least, the quest for perfection. And the consequences are not always what we expect.

In another Oriental story, we are told of a group of artists and musicians who called themselves "The Cult of Imperfection." This group called themselves this odd name because, in every piece of art or music created by the members of this group, some flaw or imperfection was deliberately incorporated. The flaws were placed in their work because they felt it was a display of audacity for anyone to try and create something perfect. They knew it could not be done, but to even try was an unthinkable act of ego. How dare anyone seek perfection! They knew that any such attempt could result in consequences that might be very unpleasant. So, their answer to the problem, and show of humility, was to create work with designed flaws.

Now, if we look at Freemasonry, we learn in the craft degrees the importance of improving yourself. The first collection of degrees in the Scottish Rite beyond the craft lodge is known as the *Lodge of Perfection*. But is the suggestion that we are really seeking perfection?

One thing we must learn about all of Masonry is that we teach with symbolism. We often find that our symbolic manner of instruction presents lessons on top of lessons. We can, of course, seek only the outer levels, and that's all we will find. But by digging deeper into the lessons, we can find so very much more.

The Scottish Rite presents us with a good example of the duality of Freemasonry. One suggestion is that this concept is outwardly represented by the double-headed eagle, or, as I believe it may have originally been, the double-headed phoenix. The thought is that the double-headed eagle (or phoenix) represents the two parts of the Scottish Rite — the organization and the philosophy. The two parts operate independently but are tied together by their roles. The philosophy remains constant and unchanged. It is the actual nature of the Scottish Rite. The organization is the human participation in and application of that philosophy. Problems begin when the two *heads* are out of sync. If there is a change or a movement in the organization away from the philosophy, then things begin to deteriorate. But is a move away from the philosophy unnatural or a preplanned and a natural part of nature's cycle?

In nature, we have four seasons. Some view these seasons as aspects of human life. Spring represents birth. Summer represents learning or growing. Fall represents passing on what we have learned to others, and Winter represents death. But then the cycle in nature begins again with another Spring. In nature, this calls in the rebirth of trees, flowers, and the beauty of the Earth. Some view this as representative of the rebirth of the human spirit following physical death.

The Rosicrucians have an old thought that anything considered of value must face the test of death. The idea is that everything positive and good must reach a point where it ceases to be as it once was and begins to fail. It begins to die. But once dead, if it is of any value to humanity, it will find a way to come back, just like the Phoenix or Spring. If it is of no value, then it will fade away and be forgotten.

We can look at aspects of this thought from the Lodge of Perfection. If we look at this body as the *Lodge of Growth*, we must recognize that only so much growth can take place. Where do you go if you are involved in the Scottish Rite's leadership and obtain every office and degree you desire? If change is unavoidable and if our steady growth has a ceiling, what does this mean? If our upward growth can go no further and change is still going to take place, then the only option for us is to come back down. Is this the death of our growth?

Death in the scenario of winter and the Rosicrucian idea of a particular test of "death" does not necessarily mean the end of something, and it does not always mean that it will happen in the blink of an eye. Death can be long and drawn out. Many hold that death begins at the moment of birth.

Death can also mean just another form of change. Individuals can belong to an organization, and if their only goal is rank, power, and authority, then there will come a time when this is no longer available. They will fall and die as a force in the organization. Unfortunately, if there are more than a few with this same attitude, then this can result in the whole organization meeting the same fate. It is one of the reasons why an organization can pull away from the philosophy.

If we look at every Masonic body — Scottish Rite, York Rite, all rites — belongs to their philosophy. The body is either in line with the philosophy (which does not change) or it is not in line. If it does not align with the basic philosophy, it begins going down. There is a thought that *going down* is part of the growth cycle and is natural. If this is the case, then it could mean that the Lodge of Perfection is designed for us to realize that we are growing to a point where we must start over again and relearn or rediscover all we have experienced. So, the concept of *going down* may not be as devastating as we might imagine.

Since the 1970s, we have heard countless reports that Masonry as a whole is declining. Yes, the Scottish Rite is also declining in some areas, and many are not attending meetings. Yet, in other areas, it is growing. I firmly believe that the Scottish Rite is going through a period of realignment in its natural cycle. I am seeing more and more young Masons joining the Scottish Rite who are not interested in the gold and silver prizes or awards that may be won. They are looking for the real gold — the teachings. And this all seems to be part of a cycle. If this is the case, then the Lodge of Perfection can hold a special place as a fundamental aspect of a continuous, never-ending cycle of esoteric education. Teachings designed to reveal new lessons with each revisiting.

The change that the Scottish Rite (and really all of Masonry) is going through now has no guarantee that it will be painless for everyone. There could be some who find this change wholly unacceptable. And we can look at an example in the world of art.

I read something not long ago about an artist who was probably more egotist than artist. He had an art show at a respected European art gallery. The show featured works by several artists, but this one artist billed himself as the main part of the show. He considered himself the new wave of modern art. He felt that the old masters were "yesterday's news." He felt that his work was far superior to theirs in quality, style, and meaning. The show went on for about a month, but the artist did not visit the galley until several weeks into the event. When he arrived at the gallery, he went directly to see the display of his newest piece and was horrified at what he saw. The gallery had hung the work upside down. They hung it this way because they had no idea which was up, and which was down. Well, the artist was furious. He began yelling that no one in the gallery had any sense of art, they were all incompetent, etc., etc. In truth, the gallery workers were all highly experienced and skilled, but the problem was that they just could not tell the direction of his work. The argument reached such a level that the gallery owner told him to take his art and leave. They replaced his art with copies of works by the old masters. In a statement made by the gallery owner, he said that if art is meaningful and understood *only* by the artist, then we need to question its value to all humanity.

And what of our organizations? If what we are doing in our various bodies is meaningful *only* to the ones who confer the degrees or run the meetings and not the general membership, then a disconnect occurs. We *must* be of value to more than a few. The Scottish Rite is a venue for the personal growth of all, not a place where only some can enjoy personal satisfaction through caps, titles, and offices. A meeting of the Lodge of Perfection is an opportunity to teach and learn the philosophy and nature of the Scottish Rite. Those who do not or cannot understand that philosophy must begin their own cycle to learn or relearn what they have forgotten or never learned. It is all part of the natural cycle of change.

What is known as the Lodge of Perfection might be better understood as the Lodge of *Perfecting*. *Perfecting* is the steady growth of the individual. It is building on what is already known to fine-tune oneself without the unrealistic goal of actually achieving perfection. And while we may obtain the highest offices and degrees, it can mean nothing as far as our personal growth. The two are not tied together. We must always continue to personally grow and *desire* to grow. We must objectively recognize when we are growing, and when we have ceased to grow. When we realize that we have stopped growing, we must look to the teachings of the Scottish Rite to begin again our own cycle of learning. We must do this without being hampered by ego or false pride. We must recognize that we are part of the whole and begin on the natural cycle with the eagerness of when we first saw the Scottish Rite degrees. It is like reading a very good book. When you are finished, sometimes you want to start all over and read it again.

Like many aspects of Masonry, the Lodge of Perfection has layers of moral philosophy built into it. We are either part of the problem or part of the solution. In this case, no one rides the fence. It is one of the consequences of the quest for perfection (improvement) which we embarked upon when we joined. So, next time you are at a Lodge of Perfection meeting, take a little time to close your eyes and just feel what is all around you. Allow yourself to be open to the deeper teachings of the ritual and the philosophy. Explore them. If you genuinely feel nothing, then try to have the strength and courage to start over. There is no shame. It is part of what growing means. Don't limit yourself to only what you must do; take the extra step. Reach out and up. It is part of what it means to be a Scottish Rite Mason.

The greatest thing in this world is not so much where we stand as in what direction we are moving.

~ Johann Wolfgang von Goethe

Guarding the West Gate

Whence came the idea that a man - almost any man - has an inherent right to become a Freemason? Is it not a privilege to be conferred upon the worthy?

~ Dwight L. Smith

We have earlier talked of the dangers faced by medieval esoteric groups who gathered in secret. The punishment for such gatherings and exploring "unacceptable" subjects could be death. But that was then, and this is now. We live in much different times and cannot be punished for privately and peacefully gathering with like-minded individuals to study obscure or even unpopular scientific, philosophical, or esoteric subjects. We have freedoms that did not exist in medieval times. So, does this mean we do not need to be concerned about who joins us? Should we open the doors of Freemasonry to anyone with only an interest? Such thoughts might display a misunderstanding of our nature and purpose for existence.

In most parts of the world, Freemasonry exists today in an atmosphere where our members do not fear for their lives simply for being a Freemason. A free society does not proscribe membership in organizations promoting morality and free thought. But we should not confuse the goals of medieval esoteric societies and modern Freemasonry. The reason for limiting memberships in the old esoteric societies was because they recognized that not everyone was suited for studying such subjects *and* for security concerns. While security is not usually an issue for Freemasonry today, it is still a fact that not everyone is suited for esoteric study — if that is the acknowledged goal of Freemasonry.

.

We may think of Freemasonry as a quality professional orchestra. Many may appreciate the music performed by the orchestra, and there may be many applications to join. But not everyone is a musician. If the orchestra allowed all interested to join, then the quality of the orchestra would diminish. With members lacking the necessary musical skills, attendance at the performances could also be expected to noticeably drop. Before long, the orchestra would cease to exist.

Freemasonry does not explicitly define morality or worth, but we do say that we only admit the worthy and that we have the goal of making good men better. We investigate candidates wishing to join and vote on their suitability to join us. But do we always understand what morality and worth mean in connection to Masonic membership? What does it mean to be worthy of membership?

The problem with understanding the nature of morality is that it can often be subjective. But there are also aspects that are universal. Murder is not viewed as moral by societies considered to be civilized, but charity is seen as an accepted moral activity. I can't imagine many disagreeing with these thoughts. But it is clear that the general concept of morality (and details of it) can change from area to area. This may explain why Freemasonry does not explicitly define morality. There are no cookie cutter answers or standard guidebooks to buy for investigation committees as each candidate and situation can be unique. An investigation committee must decide for themselves if a candidate is moral and worthy of membership using only their own standards and views of morality. Of course, they must exercise great caution and care in their judgements. To misjudge a candidate may not only be a very unfair act towards the one applying, but it may also display their own lack of morality and worth. Members of this committee have a profound responsibility.

The Investigation Committee must also not be confused when we say that Masonry is a moral institution. Masonry is for the morally fit, but it is not an "either/or" situation. If one is rejected for membership, it does not automatically mean that we are judging them as morally unfit. Being moral is a requirement for Masonic membership, but not every moral person is a proper candidate for Masonry. There are many valid reasons for rejecting a candidate that has nothing to do with morality. For example, if the wife of a petitioner objects to her husband becoming a Mason, he should be rejected for membership. In this case, the man might be wholly upright and moral, but Masonry must not interfere with family harmony. If the petitioner is married, his wife must support his initiation. If he is single and lives at home, his parents must support his becoming a Mason.

If Freemasonry is an organization designed only for the moral and worthy, and if we knowingly, or because of careless investigation, admit the immoral or unworthy (or falsely label the worthy), then Freemasonry, just like the professional orchestra, will diminish in quality. Whatever Freemasonry was at one time, there is no guarantee that it will remain so regardless of what we do or how we act. Either we are what we claim, or we are not.

The lodge investigation committee is responsible for determining a candidate's fitness for Masonic membership. But it should be recognized that the lodge's first "line of defense" is the one who signs the petition. How well did he know the candidate? It should be more than just a first meeting or a casual acquaintance. Is the one who accepts the petition a responsible brother who well knows the laws of Masonry? This, sadly, may not always be the case. I well remember when a lodge gave away a brand-new television set to whoever would bring in the most petitions. I must wonder how well those petitions were screened.

By the time the petition gets to the investigation committee (in most cases), the lodge has already voted on receiving the petition. They have shown some interest in the candidate and accepted the statements given and passed on the petition to the investigation committee for a detailed study. The system fails if no one gives any thought to the quality of the petitioner until the petition is given to an investigation committee. No petition should reach an investigation committee if anyone has any doubts about the candidate. All must do their part to ensure that none but skilled "musicians" are admitted to our Masonic "orchestra."

If we carefully consider the duties of the Investigation Committee, we can see its tremendous responsibility. The investigation committee is asked to investigate and pass judgment on the *fitness* for membership of another human being, including *moral* fitness. No considerate individual will fail to recognize the enormous responsibility being given to this committee. In my opinion, no committee has a more profound responsibility than the investigation committee. The proper performance of this committee is vitally important not only to your lodge but to the whole of Masonry.

Your lodge or Grand Lodge may provide instructions on the composition of an investigation committee. Many jurisdictions provide for a three-member committee with a Past Master as the chairman. Regardless of the composition, this committee, like others, best operates with a plan to follow. When the Worshipful Master appoints the committee, they should set a time to meet as soon as possible to begin their work. The investigation committee should thoroughly examine all available information on the petition. The last thing a lodge needs is to learn of misstatements on a petition after a petitioner has received the three degrees. The committee should then begin the task of systematically investigating all aspects of the character of the petitioner. It is incorrect to think that a comprehensive investigation is an unwarranted intrusion into the petitioner's privacy. When one seeks to join Freemasonry, Freemasonry must determine if he is worthy.

Over the last few years, a trend has been developing in several jurisdictions. Not only has there been a growing desire for new members, but an almost hunger or fervor for new members. It is easy to imagine that such a strong desire for new candidates might adversely affect the careful consideration of each petition. We must be on guard to never give the impression that the goal is merely more members, as that of a club membership drive. In such a case, an investigation committee could be viewed as more of a formality that can operate in something of a "rubber stamp" approval process. Investigations might be limited to verifying the names and addresses. That sort of practice is contrary to our teachings and detrimental to all of Freemasonry. Masonry does not need more members; Masonry needs more Masons. If we do not see the difference, then we are dooming ourselves to a slow (or quick) corruption of all for which we have stood since our creation.

It would seem that if we fail to understand the nature of something, it can often be confused with something else, leading to disastrous results. If we think of the general category of food, we can add both fish and apples to that group. If we think of the nature of a fish being the same as the nature of an apple, then we have made a serious error. They are not the same thing. Masonry can be included in a general category with many fine organizations. Specifically, however, Masonry does not operate like the Red Cross, Salvation Army, Lions Club, or any other service or charitable organization. Likewise, Masonry is not a religion and does not operate as such. We do not offer salvation or promises of aid to any and all who knock on our door. While it is true that we can often see individual Masons offering service to communities, that is not our primary goal.

Masonry has a very specific task, and that is self-improvement. The reason Past Masters are often required to be the chairman of investigation committees is because it is assumed that by the time one has become a Past Master, he should well know the exact purpose of Masonry. The experienced Past Master can lead the other members of the committee in recognizing if the petitioner is a proper fit.

Another area of confusion is religion and politics. Masons know that these are taboo subjects when a lodge is at labor. Wise Masons also avoid pointed discussions or debates of these subjects even when the lodge is at refreshment. The reason should be obvious. We all have our political opinions and religious beliefs. We recognize and respect that our faith and opinions may differ, and we also recognize that pointed discussions of these subjects might cause disharmony. But how does this affect an investigation committee? Well, being respectful of the various religious beliefs or political opinions does not mean that we do not know how our brothers feel or believe. We should know each other and still respect each other as brothers. I have heard some say that all questions concerning religion and politics should be avoided with a petitioner; that only the questions, "Do you believe in a Supreme Being?" and "Are you a citizen of this country?" should be asked. I very much disagree with this line of thinking. It was stated to me that one reason it was believed that no discussion of religion or politics should be permitted when interviewing a petitioner was in case any member of the investigation committee held biases against any particular religious faith or political party. What an incredible way of thinking! Such thinking automatically assumes that we have unworthy individuals on our committees who will unfairly evaluate petitioners! We should stop and consider this aspect with a bit of clear thinking.

We call our members "Brother," which should give us a clue as to how we should view our fellow Masons. We are members of the Masonic *family*. We need only to think of our Obligations to realize the relationship that should exist between Masons. The investigation committee is not only to investigate the character of the petitioner and his fitness for Masonry but is also a "get to know" committee. The committee members should try to learn about this individual who may soon be their brother and give the petitioner a chance to get to know the committee members. If our only interest is in the money given for the degrees, then maybe we would not care that much about getting to know the petitioner. If we are, however, investigating an individual who we might for the rest of our lives call "brother," then we should want to know all about this individual.

But does Masonry enter into the realm of religion and politics? Do we evaluate and pass judgment on religions and political parties? No. Religions and political parties are not eligible to join Masonry. Masonry admits and investigates *individuals*. Should you ask a petitioner to which religion he belongs? Unless your Grand Lodge law expressly forbids it, yes. If we do not ask pointed questions, how will we learn what should be learned? Would you be happy if someone was admitted into your lodge one who is a member of the Nazi Party or the Church of Satan? One member of an investigation committee told me that this is *exactly* what happened once when he served on this committee.

I was told of an experience where a petitioner seemed completely normal and promising. He was asked if he believed in a Supreme Being. He said yes. During a simple conversation, one of the members of the investigation committee stated that he grew up in the petitioner's neighborhood. He said that he lived near a particular church. With nothing more than general conversation in mind, he asked the petitioner if he was also a member of that church. Without hesitation, the petitioner stated that he was not and that he was a member of the Church of Satan. He then took the committee members into his "ceremony room" which was filled with satanic and pornographic paraphernalia. The brother told me that had they not asked him this simple question, he would likely have been voted into the lodge as all else seemed "routine" — from what they could tell.

At some point, common sense must be employed. If asking simple questions about a potential members religious or political belief is not allowed due to fear that it opens the door to possible persecution of the petitioner, don't we see a problem? This clearly assumes that the members of the investigation committee are unworthy Masons! "Oh, no! He's a Democrat or a Republican or a Lutheran or a Catholic! We can't let *him* in!" That's not how Masons act. If we make rules based on the belief that our own members think and act unMasonically, then we have lost before we have started.

If the nature or actions of an individual are out of line with Masonry and considered immoral to reasonable people, should we allow such an individual to join Masonry because he belongs to a religion or political party that condones such activity? No, we should not. If an investigation committee asks the religion of a petitioner, and then bases their decision on the petty unMasonic bias of the committee members, then *they* are the unworthy parties!

Today, we can find cases where some will argue that it is improper to investigate someone beyond verifying their name and address. We will find some who object to the idea of any sort of investigation of a petitioner. Make no mistake, these opinions do not serve Masonry. Freemasonry was never designed to be open to any and all. It is impossible to get into a petitioner's closed heart or mind to know their deepest secrets. No investigation committee can guarantee that an unworthy individual will not gain admission to our lodges, but we must try. We must conduct our investigations as diligently and fairly as possible. We must put the well-being of the lodge and the whole of Masonry at the forefront of our decisions and use the teachings of Masonry as our guide.

Unfortunately, no book will provide the correct answers to every possible scenario that an investigation committee can face. The members of this committee must be able to think on their feet. They must be able to take the teachings of Freemasonry and apply them to each situation they encounter. A petitioner must not be excluded for petty, external reasons (race or heritage, for example, must never be an issue). We should look only at the internal qualities of the petitioner and determine if he is a good match for our lodge. Masonry is designed to improve the good, not to make acceptable the unacceptable. We are not a reform school, an organization designed to bring trouble into a petitioner's family, or a club that accepts all with the proper payment.

Guarding the West Gate means we must welcome the worthy and keep out the unworthy. Guarding the West Gate means that we must try to learn if Masonic membership will cause problems within the family of an otherwise excellent candidate. We are not following the teachings of Freemasonry if we are unconcerned about how Masonic membership will affect a member's family. The investigation committee is to use their good common sense, diligent efforts, and the pure teachings of Masonry to guard this most important gate.

A Lodge in Need

We don't see things as they are; we see things as we are.
~ The Talmud

What do you do if you care about your lodge, but it is having trouble? Maybe the lodge is having low attendance, lack of interest, and there is a concern that the lodge is failing. Let's look at several situations and see if we can find ways to turn things around in a lodge and save a lodge that can be saved.

The first thing we should probably do is separate and identify a lodge that is actually in trouble from one that chooses to operate on a more minimalistic level. A lodge that chooses to operate on a minimalistic level would be one where there is no real plan for programs or events. Members come to lodge for a casual meal, listen to the general business of the lodge, and visit with friends. No Masonic education takes place. They simply show up for an hour or two of fellowship or, maybe, a degree every now and then. This is their interest and what they enjoy. If a lodge chooses to operate at this level, it should be their right. A lodge should not be required to change into something they may not like or appreciate. This would be especially true if what they do is working for them. Maybe the lodge members enjoy meeting in blue jeans and polo shirts. Maybe they are not interested in the deeper teachings of Freemasonry. If such is the case, then changing the lodge into something that is not desired could take a successful lodge and turn it into one that does fail.

A failing lodge is one where they do not have a quorum on more than a rare occasion. The failing lodge is one that will soon cease to exist if they do not do something to turn around their lodge in a short time.

One common problem I have seen in lodges that fail is a lack of ability to muster the interest to even learn the basics of opening and closing a lodge. While the inability of the lodge officers to properly perform the ritual is never (as far as I have seen) the sole reason for the failure of a lodge, there seems to be a building of events that do lead to the failure. In every case I have seen, the failure to properly open or close a lodge seems to be a part of the downward spiral of a lodge. It would seem that this is part of the overall dissatisfaction with the lodge or a growing lack of caring about any aspect of lodge operation. Once a lodge starts down the path of not caring, it is tough to turn things around.

One thing that we should also consider is that everything in the universe exists in cycles. There is a natural cycle for everything, including lodges. While in most cases, a lodge is simply sick and not actually dying, we must realize that sometimes, no matter what we do or attempt to change, a lodge will have gone so far down that there is no bringing it back. If we see that a lodge is, in fact, in the process of dying, then we should contact the Grand Lodge for assistance. The Grand Lodge can assist the lodge and its members — maybe the lodge could merge with another lodge. The Grand Lodge also has procedures for handling any assets the lodge may have in case it decides to fold up and turn in its charter.

Fortunately, most of the time, a lodge is more on the side of being sick than dying, and there are things that we can do to correct the sickness before it destroys the lodge. One of the simple things to change in a lodge is the manner of perception, or how we perceive and project ourselves as a lodge. This can take the form of how we perform our rituals, how we dress, the condition of our lodge, how we act in lodge, and the meals we serve before lodge. All of these elements add to the overall perception of worth.

Value is subjective. This cannot be stated enough. I recently saw someone on the news who bought a painting at a garage sale for 50 cents. They then sold the same painting in an auction for $10,000. One person perceived its value as almost nothing, it was only trash. But another saw the true value of the painting. What we must never do is undervalue ourselves. Even the most modest Masonic lodge is of great value and worthy of the work needed to save it.

When we go about repairing or curing a sick lodge, the first thing we should do is objectively evaluate the lodge, its members, and all aspects of the working of the lodge. We need to properly understand where we are so that we can make positive changes.

We must never fail to understand the importance of perception. In addition to the story about the 50-cent painting that sold for thousands, there is a report that Amazon conducted an experiment a few years back with artwork by some of the world's great masters. The paintings were not identified as being by the masters, and the suggestion was that they were done by new artists and offered for evaluation by the viewers. The suggested price for each painting was about $500.00. The vast majority of the comments made were negative. Most of the viewers were not aware that what they were evaluating was very significant works of art, and, as such, they judged the paintings harshly. Appearance and perception are very important, and it says something no matter if we want it to or not.

The Amazon experiment (regardless of *why* viewers felt as they did—something better answered by sociologists or physiologists) teaches us that qualities such as beauty and value vary from person to person. People often like things based on perception. Many times, we like something if everyone else likes it. If *they* don't like something, then we also fall in line. It is far easier to like something new if it is attached to someone or something famous. If you don't recognize some aspect of what you are looking at, then something new often must live up to higher expectations. Discounting these human traits when offering something to others can result in disappointment.

We must understand that the image we project means something. How we are perceived means something. If it is the custom of the members of our lodge to dress in blue jeans and polo shirts and operate the lodge in a more casual manner, that's fine. If it works for the lodge, then this is great. All is well if what we are doing works for us. But, if things are not going so well for the lodge, if we want more, or if we see the need for any improvement, then we need to look at our image.

If our lodge is in trouble, then the first step is to change how we view ourselves—the lodge. The lodge meeting should be viewed as a special event. Going to lodge should not be the twice a month drudgery. It should be something special in our lives. The lodge officers should take the extra step to clean up and dress up before coming to lodge. A coat and tie are preferable, but at the very least, nice shirt and slacks should be worn. By dressing up, the members will be taking extra steps before leaving home for the lodge. Inside their minds, they will realize that they are performing these extra tasks because the lodge is worth it. A perception of worth and value is created.

Another very important aspect to consider in helping a sick lodge is for the officers to learn the short ritual of the opening and closing of the lodge. I do not mean making sure that the one guy who knows the ritual is there to feed you a good many of the words. I mean *you* knowing the ritual so that you are comfortable with it and can do it with few, if any, errors. There is no excuse for the lodge's officers not to know the simple opening and closing ritual. If someone is incapable of learning, by heart, the ritual of the opening and closing, then he should not be an officer of the lodge. It is as simple as that. Everyone wants to go through the chairs and be a Past Master, but it should not be expected if one cannot learn the work. The best interest of the lodge must be placed first. I have seen some lodges where multiple officers must be fed nearly every second word of the ritual. It creates a very negative atmosphere in the lodge.

An old bit of folk humor goes, "The way to a man's heart is through his stomach." There is truth to that statement! Lodges that serve meals should take note. Showing up at lodge for a dinner of hot dogs regularly can wear thin. If you are going to serve meals, then some care and thought should be made as to what meals to serve. Like everything else in the lodge, some forethought and planning should be made for the menu. A good stand-by is covered dish night. It is a very enjoyable and, if planned right, cost-effective event. The Worshipful Master should have a list of the regular members, and all should be called to see who will bring which dish. A master list of main dishes, side dishes, and desserts should be made so that you do not end up with 20 desserts and no main course. If the lodge has a kitchen where meals can be prepared, then plan the meals with as much care as any event is planned. Humans enjoy eating with others in social settings. Make the meals of the lodge as unique and enjoyable as possible.

If you act or look unprofessional, that is how you will be perceived. If the officers of a lodge look like they don't know what they are doing, or, worse yet, if they look like they don't care about what they are doing, this will be the message delivered to the members and visitors. If you don't care, they won't care. This impression will give the members a perfect reason to look for something else to do on lodge night.

If you belong to a lodge in trouble and you are in a leadership position, then you have a choice. Either you do what is needed to change how things are done in your lodge and the direction you are taking, or you choose to do nothing. If you choose to change, you must be willing to do what it takes to make the change happen. The fact is that many times

Masons with interest or potential are grabbed quickly and pushed into positions that they are not seasoned enough to hold. They become Worshipful Master of their lodge before they really understand Masonry. This is a fact. To these young Masons who are drafted into positions quickly after your raising, I must point out that if you accept a position in a lodge, you have accepted a *responsibility* to the lodge. Being inexperienced does not relieve you of this responsibility. I strongly suggest that you take the time to understand not only what it means to be a Mason but what it means to be a lodge officer. Even if some become upset with you, don't allow yourself to be pushed into something for which you don't feel prepared.

If you are new to Masonry, if your lodge seems to be in trouble, and if you are given an office soon after your raising, then you need to stop and think for a moment. Masonic lodges that are operating properly should not be in trouble. If your lodge is in trouble, then chances are it has been operating improperly for some time. If you reach this conclusion, then you are at the point where you must stop and carefully consider where the logic of the situation is taking you.

The leadership of your lodge (including the officers and the Past Masters who advise them) may all be friends and truly good Masons. But, if you are serious about fixing or turning around your lodge, you must understand that the lodge is in its present situation because of what the present and past leadership did or did not do. Being a *nice guy* does not mean that you possess good judgment or are a good leader. You must also realize that the same flawed judgment that has resulted in the lodge being in its present state has resulted in *you* now being in a position of the present or future leadership of the lodge. What can or will you do with that information?

Whatever good or poor judgment resulted in your being offered a position, once you accept it, you have accepted a responsibility to the lodge. What you do with that responsibility is your choice. No one else can be blamed for any poor choices you make. You are a Master Mason. If you have not learned what you need to know to properly hold an office, then you need to learn whatever you lack. Who you seek to learn from is also a matter of choice and judgment.

Think about it. As good a group of guys as they may be, you must realize that it was under *their* watch that the lodge fell or did not turn around. Whatever they did or did not do contributed to the present situation. Are *they* the ones from whom you should seek counsel on how to turn around the lodge? Of course not.

If you seek to break the downward spiral of a lodge, then you must step outside the lodge for guidance in turning things around. You cannot expect sound advice on turning around a lodge from those who have only participated in a failing lodge. You also do not wish to rub the lodge's failure in the faces of the present and past leadership. But, in the end, fresh perspectives and ideas are necessary.

Visit lodges that you know are successful. Look at how they operate and all aspects of their operation. Ask questions of the officers and members. Try to find out what they are doing and compare it with your lodge. Buy books that have Masonic lodge operation, improvement, or practices as a subject. Make use of the internet to find the available educational tools.

If your lodge is minimalistic and you are not successful, then dress up for lodge, learn the ritual, and introduce programs with Masonic education as the subject. Plan out the year, not just something for the next meeting. Lay out a plan (even if only a few months at a time) so that the time does not slip away from you. Stay in contact with the membership. I know of one brother who, within one year, had two major surgeries, and no one from the lodge even so much as sent him a get-well card. The lodge's attitude was that if you did not come to meetings, it was *your* fault if the lodge forgot about you. What a sorry attitude.

The number of ways you can save a lodge by far outnumbers the number of things that will cause a lodge to fail. Lodges die from apathy. Members may not be interested in what you are doing. Be bold. Try *this*, and if it does not work, try *that*. Make them interested. Be open and clear. Lay the situation clearly on the line for the members. Make it clear to the members that you care. If members and visitors see officers in old clothes lounging in their stations, yelling out at others from all over the place, then they realize that the officers are not professional or maybe don't care. Clean up your act. Be professional. In every case, please take what you have and make the most of it. Ensure the grass is cut and the hall is clean and clutter-free. Open the windows and air the place out. Freshen up the place. The appearance of the lodge should make members proud. A modest lodge is OK, a dirty lodge is not.

Several officers of like mind can turn around a lodge in a short time. The key is dedication and the ability to be creative. Do not repeat what has been done in the past. It's a new day. Make a new plan.

If you don't know where you are going,
you'll end up someplace else.

~ Yogi Berra

The Cup of Coffee

I don't like that man. I must get to know him better.
~ Abraham Lincoln

Human beings are intensely curious creatures who often delight in figuring out puzzles. But if the puzzle becomes too difficult to solve as quickly as they may desire, their curiosity is sometimes tempered by bouts of angry frustration. "There is no answer!" or "any ole answer will do" if the solution is not quick in arriving. Sometimes the puzzle is placed on the side with the promise to return to it "when the time is right." Rocks will become water before that happens.

One of the great puzzles in life is our fellow human beings. "What's that guy really like?" "Is he my friend or someone who I should worry about?" What do we know of the person behind the face we recognize or the name we know? Who is he deep inside, and what are his values, beliefs, and thoughts? How often have we been disappointed or even shocked when news of a major scandal is reported concerning an entertainer or politician who we like or respect? We often feel a sense of personal betrayal when it is shown that they are nothing as we believed. But why? We must realize that if all we know about someone is their name or face, then that is *all* we know about them. We certainly have the right to believe anything we like, but we do ourselves no favors when we confuse opinions with facts. We don't truly know someone if all we know is superficial.

Regardless of everything, we do sometimes form opinions about others with little to no support. What we believe about another, good or bad, can become almost as strong as a religious belief. We *know* this or that to be the true nature of someone because ... well, because we *know* it. To change our minds is often unthinkable. Khalil Gibran wrote, "Faith is a knowledge within the heart, beyond the reach of proof." Some say that pride keeps us from accepting the truth about someone when we have a long-held contrary opinion. We *need* to believe whatever we believe, or it will somehow make us seem less than we would like to be seen. Another thought is that deep seeded insecurities cause us to hold onto unsupported beliefs about others.

English philosopher, Basil Mitchell, offers us an insightful parable concerning unsupported opinions when meeting a stranger during wartime:

"In time of war in an occupied country, a member of the resistance meets one night a stranger who deeply impresses him. The partisan is utterly convinced at that meeting of the stranger's sincerity and constancy and undertakes to trust him. They never meet in conditions of intimacy again. But sometimes the stranger is seen helping members of the resistance, and the partisan is grateful and says to his friends, 'He is on our side.' Sometimes he is seen in the uniform of the police handing over patriots to the occupying power. On these occasions his friends murmur against him: but the partisan still says, 'He is on our side.' He still believes that, in spite of appearances, the stranger did not deceive him... Sometimes his friends, in exasperation, say, 'Well, what would he have to do for you to admit that you were wrong and that he is not on our side?' But the partisan refuses to answer."

Opinions like religious beliefs do not have to be intellectually convincing. Faith is of such a nature that we can justify matters of trust or views with nothing tangible to support them. In Mitchell's parable, how much evidence is required to show that the stranger has betrayed the resistance fighter? There is no simple answer to this question — but Mitchell shows us that it is reasonable to give the stranger the benefit of the doubt. The parable would equally work if the stranger were mistrusted even though others saw actions to give cause to trust him. We sometimes believe things about others simply because we want to believe them. We can *feel* something inside of us and go with it. Trusting our feelings is unprovable but has at times saved lives. We can't discount it. But is there a better way to form opinions of others?

And what of our lodge brothers? Do we really know someone who we see, at best, only once or twice a month? Does knowing where they live, and their wife and children's names mean we *know* them? If the honest answer to that question is that we really don't know our lodge brothers, then the next question must be, why not? Why don't we *know* someone who we call *brother*?

If we stop and think about it, maybe we should not be so shocked that we do not know our brothers and neighbors so very well. If we are truthful with ourselves, do we even really know ourselves? Or do we just exist on the surface, going about our daily lives and tasks with little thought of who or what we or others are all about deep inside? Many accept life and all that goes with it as a single slice of time where we do things that promote the best chances of what we feel is an acceptable existence and give no deeper thought to much of anything else.

If life is all about working to build a better life, to gain titles, notice, and worldly treasures, then we need to stop and think for a moment. If this is our thinking, doesn't it seem a bit foolish when we are doing so in a body that is in a state of perpetual decay? Don't we realize that we are structuring our lives for an ultimate end to the usefulness of this physical form? And if so, why *should* we try to understand ourselves or those around us? Why bother trying to understand what is ultimately falling apart? Why not just do what we can to make life simpler? Well, the truth is that simpler is not always better.

Surprise, we are human. With our humanity goes all the good and the bad. Human nature is something that any thoughtful person must deal with at some point if we wish for any sort of peace of mind. It is human nature to take the shorter, simpler path. If we can avoid something unpleasant, we will. If given a choice, how many kids would eat vegetables rather than ice cream? If we could avoid (or minimize) consequences, many of us would be willing to act selfishly because our goal is to make the moment easier. We often don't wish to consider the future as it may never come to pass. But human nature is not always our friend.

The attitude of *thinking about the moment and hoping for the best* is one that so very often comes back to bite us when the future does come around. Regret for wasted time or missed opportunities can come into our lives, even privately, and we waste even more time dealing with that painful emotion. There is much more to life and living than the easy, simple path.

There is something inside us all that speaks in a voice that we know but may not always want to hear and often misunderstand. We can think of it as the "inner voice," conscience, spirit, or any other form of "self" that can make us comfortable or not. In silence, we can sometimes have moments of clarity that give us answers that may have been rejected at other times. It's not all "me." It is "us." But how can it be "us" if we don't understand or know the "other"? For that matter, are we sure that we understand ourselves? Jesus is quoted as saying, "Physician, heal thyself." (Luke 4:23) We need to know ourselves before we can hope to know others. We need to correct our own defects before we speak of the defects of others.

A simple cup of coffee with another can open doors we may not even know existed. Sitting down with someone and talking is of tremendous value — and I don't mean chat, I mean *talk*. We need to dig deep, ask questions, and answer them. Learn what the other thinks, what they believe about things, and what they like and dislike. Learn all we can about that person sitting across from us.

Of course, we are free to believe anything we choose, but if we truly seek enlightenment, don't we want to base our beliefs on more than outward suggestions? We advance, step by step, through a process of education. We learn the truth; we don't guess it.

It is a new day, and it brings new opportunities. There are many sorrows in this world over which we have no control, but we have total control over what we think and how we act. We can control ourselves. We can try to understand our fellow man, our brothers. We can sit down, have a cup of coffee with someone and try to really *talk* with them — before it is too late.

A Young Man Joins a Masonic Lodge

(Preview Chapter from
Measured Expectations
By Michael R. Poll)

Not long ago, a young man turned in his petition to a Masonic lodge. Maybe a relative of his was a Mason, or maybe he learned of Freemasonry from a popular book or movie. Regardless, he expressed his desire to join.

A few weeks after turning in his petition, he received a phone call from a man who told him that he was a member of an investigation committee working on the petition. He asked the young man if he and two other lodge members could come to his house to meet with him. They met at the appointed time. It was a good meeting. Questions were asked, and everyone learned a bit more of each other.

The committee told the young man that Freemasonry is not an insurance agency. Masonry does not extend health benefits nor give promises of financial aid. While lodges and individual Freemasons have a long and honorable history of assisting those in need, Freemasonry is not designed to be a charitable organization, such as the Red Cross.

Freemasonry is also not a civic association such as the Jaycees or Lions Club. The primary goal of Freemasonry is to take good men and, through moral instruction, give them the keys by which they can, hopefully, make themselves better and happier in their lives.

The young man took in all that he was told. He then asked about the history of Freemasonry. He was told that we don't have a complete or clear understanding of all aspects of our beginnings. We know that we are old. As an organization, we go back to around 1717 with the reported creation of the Grand Lodge of England. But many claim that we can trace ourselves to much earlier times — to the days of the old Operative Freemasons. Many also claim that we can trace our philosophy and manner of symbolic education to an even much earlier time. Sadly, we just don't have definitive answers. The young petitioner accepted all that he was told, and the committee left. Both sides were satisfied.

The young man was quietly excited. He knew that what he wanted to join was something very old and very important. He couldn't explain why, but he felt it in his heart. He had done his homework. He had already read the popular books and conducted internet searches of Freemasonry. He knew better than to pay attention to the large amount of flash concerning Freemasonry. He ignored the wild supernatural claims and nonsensical satanic charges. But he knew that there was something very special about Freemasonry, its manner of instruction by degrees, and the whole Masonic philosophy. He felt very good about joining.

In a few weeks, a letter came in the mail telling him that the lodge had voted on his petition. The ballot was clear, and the date of the initiation set. But there were many questions that he had forgotten to ask. One thing that he was unsure about was how he should dress for the initiation. He thought about calling, but then remembered some of the books he owned. In them the Masons all wore business suits and some even wore tuxedoes. The photos were not particularly old, so he thought that he should try to match their dress. He knew that this was something special but assumed that if they wanted him to wear a tuxedo, they would have told him. So, he decided to wear his suit.

When he showed up at the lodge, a number of the members were wearing old blue jeans and equally faded and worn polo shirts — some t-shirts. Others looked like they were wearing soiled work clothes and had come directly to lodge from work. He felt a bit out of place in such a casual atmosphere. One of the men laughed when he saw him and asked if he was going to church or a wedding.

The young man waited downstairs and was finally called up for the initiation. He felt slightly uncomfortable as the man who came down for him was laughing and told him, "Now you are in for it!" In for what? What did he mean by that?

He was placed in a little room by a kindly, elderly man who seemed sincerely interested in his well-being. This made him feel better. The degree began.

After the degree ended, the young man had mixed emotions. He knew that what he had experienced was something very important, but why was there so much laughter and talking going on? Why did he hear a considerable amount of yelling out instructions? It was clear that some who spoke did not, at all, know their lines (they were stumbling and fumbling over every few words) and others, from everywhere, were telling the officers what to say (and, loudly).

As he was walking around, he also heard about someone's wife being sick and another's cousin who is building a new garage. What did all that have to do with his degree? But afterwards, everyone was so friendly. Maybe he expected too much. Maybe Freemasonry really is just a group of men who meet to enjoy themselves and try to do antiquated and meaningless ritual every now and then.

In time, the young man's feelings about Masonry changed from those prior to his joining. These were all nice guys. Every time he went to a meeting, he was greeted with smiles, friendly handshakes, and inquiries of his health and well-being.

There was a mixture of blue-collar workers and professional men. All seemed truly interested in the lodge, but most could not really answer even the most basic questions concerning Freemasonry. It was almost as if Freemasonry and the lodge were two completely different things.

Questions on the ritual or history were always passed to one brother who they said was the "answer man." They were a nice group of men — friends — but there was nothing *special* in the lodge; special in the way he viewed Masonry before he joined. This was a club made up of good guys who would meet a couple of times a month to enjoy themselves. They would visit and share a few laughs during a friendly evening. That seemed to be all that he could expect from the lodge experience. The books clearly were speaking of something else. But what? Who were the Freemasons that he had read about? Did they ever exist? Was it all made up to sell books?

After a few months, the young man found that a TV show was scheduled at the same time as his lodge meeting. It was a show that he had wanted to watch for some time. He chose the show over the lodge. Over the next few months and years, it became easier and easier to choose many events over the lodge meetings.

Eventually, the young man attended lodge, maybe, once, or twice a year. He made an effort to try to attend some of the important meetings. He did so out of a feeling of obligation, not really enjoyment. He did see some who truly seemed to enjoy each and every meeting. These were the men who kept the lodge alive.

At a few meetings, some of the ones who were always there gently scolded him for not attending more of the lodge functions. "You know, the lodge depends on its members and if you don't support the lodge, it will fail." But what was he to do? Was he really obligated to continually go to a place that provided him with no benefit at all other than a few laughs and a meal? He had tried, but after many months of only hearing a reading of the last meeting, bills that needed to be paid, who was sick, and discussion of the next planned social event, he grew disinterested. He knew that he could spend his time in more productive ways.

So, was he to be blamed as it was suggested? He even read such things from "ranking" Masons who seemed to put all responsibility for the success or failure of a body on his simply attending, regardless of what was offered. The man at the top was never to blame, and even if he was, nothing was ever done. There was no accountability for poor leadership. It was always the rank and file members who seemed to be the responsible parties.

The suggestion was that there was some lacking in the young Mason, and he needed to "wake up" then give his total support to whatever was offered.

Was there a lacking in him?

Freemasonry either failed this young man in about every way possible or there truly was some lacking in him. Was there a misunderstanding on his part as to the actual nature of Freemasonry? Is Freemasonry only a club made up of good men who try to do charitable work and hold friendly meetings, or is it an organization designed to educate and uplift its members through moral instruction?

In several publications, the young man saw written: "Freemasonry is the world's oldest and largest fraternity. Its history and tradition date to antiquity. Its singular purpose is to make good men better."

Okay, that's clear. But how do we do that?

Since this quote was written in a Masonic education publication, maybe that should give us a clue. We should teach and instruct our candidates. There are countless books and articles written on Masonic education. We learn the importance of education and teaching in our very ritual. But apart from the ritual, do we actually *teach* Freemasonry, or is it only words to be spoken or read and not acted upon?

How many young men are lost to us simply because we fail to do what we say we will do?

William Lowe Bryan (the tenth president of Indiana University) is credited with writing: "Education is one of the few things a person is willing to pay for and not get." This is sometimes very true, and has been for a good number of years, regarding Freemasonry. It seems that the hole that was left when quality education ceased to take place in the lodges may have been replaced with added fellowship.

That's not a bad thing, but it's not the life blood of Freemasonry. Initiation and making good men "better" is our main reason for existence.

The passing of time is unavoidable. Every year, our lodges hold elections for officers to lead them for the next year. The young men who came into the lodge, but learned very little about Freemasonry, are now in leadership positions. They are the leaders, but truthfully, many are not qualified.

To be fair, it's not really their fault. With the speed many of them go through the chairs, how can they help but be inexperienced? They are where they are because someone tapped them on the shoulder and asked them if they would accept a position. They were just trying to be helpful.

Maybe the lodge felt that it had no one else to ask and had to take whoever it could get. Maybe it was felt that to take anyone, even someone very inexperienced, was better than closing shop.

Where Masonic education once took place, discussions of lodge picnics or other lodge events are heard at the meetings. The time that was once spent by the Worshipful Master on the planning of the Masonic education of the members is often now spent on trying to learn the very basics of lodge leadership.

Lodge meetings are only as long as felt necessary and then the "enjoyable" time of the lodge takes place — sharing a few laughs with friends. The leaders are expected to keep the members happy, not spend too much money, and get through their year with as little hassle as possible. The "hole" was filled, and we are marking time, just getting through the years.

But marking time and just getting by does not secure the future of Freemasonry. It is not responsible. It is not enough that we *say* that we are "Freemasonry," but act like a club. We must either be what we say or admit to being something else.

To all the junior officers of Freemasonry, no matter if you are brand new to Freemasonry, or have been a Mason for a number of years and are only now returning to lodge activity; no matter what level of experience and knowledge you have — *stop*. Take a breath. You are not alone. You don't have to have a situation where young men are leaving your lodges because of claims that you are not giving them what they expected. You don't have to worry that you will all of a sudden be in charge and not know what in the world to do or say. You have Brothers who wish to help you.

But just as each of you had to step up and ask to join Freemasonry, you need to step up and make your needs and desires known. And when you are a junior officer is the time when you should do this.

The internet is filled with Masonic education websites, but which are reliable? You may wish to seek out the recognized and respected Masonic education sources. In the U.S., quality Masonic educational/service societies which you can, and should, join such as The Philalethes Society;[1] The Masonic Society;[2] The Masonic Service Association of North America[3] and other worthy state and national organizations are designed to provide quality Masonic educational resources and services.

I believe deeply in the importance of finding balance in everything. Going too far one way or the other never seems to bring about what is truly desired. But what do we do about our present situation? We have already gone too far. Our lodges have taken on more of the appearance of clubs than lodges of moral instruction.

It was not done through maliciousness; it was done out of a desire to help and preserve. It did not happen all at once, but over a period of time. It was done with no ill intentions. We all know that there is a problem in our lodges. We know that they are not the same lodges as before.

We hear the stories of days long gone. Our leaders desire to do good, but some are uncertain as to which path is the best one. None wish for everything to fall apart on their watch. Some may feel that to do nothing is better than to do the wrong thing.

But cancer is never cured by inaction. There is an old Rosicrucian thought that everything felt to be of value must face the test of death. What is truly of value, will come back alive. What is of no value, will fade away.

Is Freemasonry of value?

I do not believe that society (or any group of people) is changed in mass by outside influences. I believe that change always comes through individual change. When we change as individuals, and if others change in a like manner, then society changes. I believe that the very first step we can take is to recognize that we are in trouble and traveling in the wrong direction.

Value is a perception. We place whatever value we choose on something. Value can also change. If you don't treat something as if it is special or valuable, it's not.

Anyone who knows me personally knows that I live in blue jeans. But those who only know me from lodge believe that I live in business suits. Going to lodge is something very special to me. I dress accordingly. If I did not own a suit, I would clean myself and then put on the best shirt and slacks that I owned.

Try this the next time you visit your lodge: act as if it is a *very* special occasion; as if you are going to a *very* special place to do *very* special things. Do what you would do if you were going to such a special event.

Fix your mind to always treat going to lodge as something *very* important and special. Make that one permanent change in your life. After you have done this, join or take advantage of what is offered in one of the Masonic education services or societies mentioned earlier.

Freemasonry will be what its members make it. The true and sole power within Freemasonry is where it has always been, with its members — with you.

Notes:

1. http://www.freemasonry.org/
2. http://themasonicsociety.com/
3. http://www.msana.com/

About The Author

Michael R. Poll (1954 - present) is the owner of Cornerstone Book Publishers and former editor of the *Journal of The Masonic Society*. He is a Fellow and Past President of The Masonic Society, a Fellow of the Philalethes Society, a Fellow of the Maine Lodge of Research, Member of the Society of Blue Friars, and Full Member of the Texas Lodge of Research.

A New York Times Bestselling writer and publisher, he is a prolific writer, editor, and publisher of Masonic and esoteric books. He is also the host of the YouTube channel "New Orleans Scottish Rite College."

As time permits, he travels and speaks on the history of Freemasonry, with a particular focus on the early history of the Scottish Rite.

He was born in New Orleans, LA and lives a peaceful life with his wife and two sons.

More Masonic Books from Cornerstone

Robert's Rules of Order: Masonic Edition
Revised by Michael R. Poll
6 x 9 Softcover 212 pages
ISBN 1887560076

In His Own (w)Rite
by Michael R. Poll
6×9 Softcover 176 pages
ISBN: 1613421575

Measured Expectations
The Challenges of Today's Freemasonry
by Michael R. Poll
6×9 Softcover 180 pages
ISBN: 978-1613422946

A Masonic Evolution
The New World of Freemasonry
by Michael R. Poll
6×9 Softcover 176 pages
ISBN: 978-1-61342-315-8

An Encyclopedia of Freemasonry
by Albert Mackey
Revised by William J. Hughan and Edward L. Hawkins
Foreword by Michael R. Poll
8.5 x 11, Softcover 2 Volumes 960 pages
ISBN 1613422520

Cornerstone Book Publishers
www.cornerstonepublishers.com

More Masonic Books from Cornerstone

Our Stations and Places - Masonic Officer's Handbook
by Henry G. Meacham
Revised by Michael R. Poll
6 x 9 Softcover 164 pages
ISBN: 1887560637

Masonic Enlightenment
The Philosophy, History and Wisdom of Freemasonry
Edited by Michael R. Poll
6 x 9 Softcover 180 pages
ISBN 1887560750

10,000 Famous Freemasons
4 Vol. Softcover Edition
by William Denslow
Foreword by Harry S. Truman
Cornerstone Foreword by Michael R. Poll
8.5 x 11, Softcover 2 Volumes 1,515 pages
ISBN 1887560319

The Freemason's Monitor
by Thomas Smith Webb
6×9 Softcover 316 pages
ISBN: 1613422717

The Bonseigneur Rituals
A Rare Collection of 18th Century New Orleans Ecossais Rituals
Edited by Gerry L. Prinsen
Foreword by Michael R. Poll
8x10 Softcover 2 volumes 574 pages
ISBN 1934935344

Cornerstone Book Publishers
www.cornerstonepublishers.com

New Orleans Scottish Rite College

www.youtube.com/c/NewOrleansScottishRiteCollege

Clear, Easy to Watch
Scottish Rite and Craft Lodge
Podcast & Video Education

www.ingramcontent.com/pod-product-compliance
Lightning Source LLC
Chambersburg PA
CBHW031127020426
42333CB00012B/265